World Tales for Family Storytelling II

44 Traditional Stories
for Children
aged 6–8 years

World Tales for Family Storytelling II © Storytelling Schools Ltd

Chris Smith is hereby identified as the author of this work in accordance with section 77 of the Copyright, Designs and Patent Act, 1988. He asserts and gives notice of his moral right under this Act.

Published by Hawthorn Press, Hawthorn House,
1 Lansdown Lane, Stroud, Gloucestershire, GL5 1BJ, UK
Tel: (01453) 757040 E-mail: info@hawthornpress.com
Website: www.hawthornpress.com

Illustrations © Shirin Adl
Cover design by Lucy Guenot
Typesetting by Winslade Graphics
Printed by Henry Ling Ltd, The Dorset Press

Printed on environmentally friendly chlorine-free paper sourced from renewable forest stock.

Every effort has been made to trace the ownership of all copyrighted material. If any omission has been made, please bring this to the publisher's attention so that proper acknowledgement may be given in future editions.

The views expressed in this book are not necessarily those of the publisher.

British Library Cataloguing in Publication Data applied for

ISBN 978-1-912480-66-1

Storytelling Series

World Tales for Family Storytelling II

44 Traditional Stories for Children
aged 6–8 years

Chris Smith

Foreword by Georgiana Keable

Hawthorn Press

Contents

Stories

Foreword

Confession time. I usually skip the foreword and read it later only if I really like a book. Maybe you've already laughed or cried, chuckled or thoroughly enjoyed this wonderful collection of *World Tales* for six to eight year olds. Perhaps like me you are well above the age group. If, however you haven't yet dipped into the book, you are in for a treat.

I'm an old hand in this game, I've been a full-time storyteller for most of my adult life. My earnings have been miserably small compared to an average Norwegian but it has never bothered me as the payment in joy and wonder is beyond banking. Here, in this book are the tools to earn yourself these kinds of priceless rewards. Large sparkling six-year-old eyes gazing at you, or through you into a parallel world of wonder and wisdom. Perhaps one of these young listeners will say, 'Again!' Or that other stamp of a good story told – 'Is that really true?' Despite flying horses, speaking frogs or invisibility cloaks, if one enters that parallel world together, a kind of truth rings out.

This is our invisible cultural heritage, passed down generations by ordinary people like you and I for free. It is outside the market economy and yet hidden in its picture language are the secrets of how to live together with other humans and with the living world. Not moralistically pressed into lectures or lessons but painted into stories imbued with wonder.

I started storytelling with Ben Haggarty and Tuup in mainly Asian and Black primary schools in West London in the early 1980s. Most of the children in our audiences had never experienced live storytelling before. And yet, strangely, it was as if they recognised this form of transmission at once. At the time teachers had a new catch phrase. We were regularly warned that children, particularly boys, suffered from 'short attention spans'. Strangely this never seemed to affect our storytelling.

Children were packed in and we often had six or even seven shows a day. But their attention spans had magically stretched and at times it even seemed like the usually 'difficult' ones understood this art form better. At this time we thought ourselves the first ones to rediscover the immense fun and power of stories. Children often ran up and hugged us as a spontaneous thanks. As time passed a strange thing happened. It became clearer and clearer that many people all over the world had in one way or another stumbled into this gold-mine of communication.

Simultaneously another mystery appeared. Why was it that I met storytellers from other parts of the UK, from the far reaches of Europe, even from other continents who told many of the same stories that we were telling. At that moment almost none of us were published and in those ancient pre-internet days we usually met in person. Why had we chosen to tell so many of the same tales? As time passes I conclude that this is because some stories transcend the test of time. In this book Chris Smith has collected and retold many of these tales. The twin genius of this collection is that Chris tells them with bold clear pictures so that they are easy to learn and then to develop and pass on.

But there is a vital element to this book which is do-it-yourself! You can read these stories aloud and they will work. But that magic, that powerful shared experience where an audience of one child, or your family, wakes to live and breathe with you the strange and wondrous events of a parallel world is something more. In order for that to happen you will need to ignite your imagination. After 20 years of teaching at Oslo University and holding countless courses for children and adults, I can vouch 100 percent that this mysterious faculty lies within us all. There is no-one that I have come across who won't enjoy the transformation of making a story their own.

I remember an older woman, let us call her Martina, who really took against a story I had given her to tell. It's the tale of the *The Happy Man's Shirt* which most people really like, so I was surprised and offered her another one. But although she disliked it she decided to stick to the story and went through the imaginative process along with everyone else. In the beginning of *The Happy Man's Shirt*, a king's son is so very ill that they fear for his life and it's prophesied that the only thing that can save him is to wear the shirt of a truly happy man. They look and look, but it turns out to be very hard to find a happy man and when at last they do find him, alas he has no shirt on!

Martina at last told the story very beautifully. But she changed the ending, instead of leaving the son to die through the lack of a shirt from a happy man, the prince took off his shirt too and was cured at once. Then Martina told us that she had lost her only and deeply beloved child so when she read the ending, where it seemed the king's son would die, it was just too painful to bear. But then her imagination kicked in and she found a deep joy in having the power to give life to the young prince. She said she had grown by facing her loss once again. And of course, for us the listeners the story became moving far beyond its usual capacity.

Just as we want to feed our children well, we can nourish them with stories, and in this book you will find a great larder of tastes both sweet and sour. When we moved to Norway with our children aged five, eight and eleven, they were a pretty happy bunch but they couldn't speak Norwegian. They were plonked into classes with a full Norwegian timetable, different norms and friendship groups. It was hard, not to say traumatic and one of them began to say she didn't want to carry on living, while the youngest refused to learn Norwegian and carried on in English regardless for the first year. Our financial situation was as usual dire and we moved to a little hut in the woods, which was cheap and turned out to be both illegal and in danger of flooding but seemed like a great adventure. However it was an area where they weren't used to newcomers and someone put fireworks in our postbox. Two neighbour girls from a very well-off family came to play in the little wood outside the cottage and picked violets in the garden but said they would never have such a messy lawn like that at home.

At the end of that hard first year there was a storytelling festival for adults. This was something the children were used to and the two youngest won the lying competition hands down. The prize was several cardboard boxes filled with chocolate which had been donated to the festival. As they seldom saw chocolate at home they were of course delighted. That night Duncan Williamson the legendary Scottish traveller who has meant so much for the storytelling revival in Scotland and the UK, came to stay with us for the night. Duncan, who didn't seem to eat ordinary food but who seemed to survive on very strong sweet tea and cigarettes, got on like a house on fire with our girls. We stayed up all night telling stories. I don't remember which stories Duncan told but this meeting seemed like a massive injection of courage for the children. At that time the tide turned and they began to thrive. You never really know but it seemed to me the stories fed them with the courage and resilience they needed to meet a new country. However maybe it was really just the chocolate.

I wish you and your children much enjoyment from this splendid collection. May the stories grow wings in your mind and spread joy on the trill of your tongue!

Georgiana Keable, storyteller and author of *The Natural Storyteller*

Introduction

Storytelling in the home is a tried and tested way of helping your family to thrive. Since the dawn of language, humans have shared stories together in their families and tribes as a way of sharing information, learning language and bonding as a group. Our minds are hardwired to enjoy such story sharing. Some would say that our survival has depended on it.

What is meant by storytelling? In this volume the stories are intended to be told by an adult to a child or children, told jointly with the children joining in in various ways, or told independently by the child to an adult or to other children in the family. The main idea is to retell them from memory in the storyteller's own words, rather than read them out word-for-word although the stories can also be read if you wish.

Such storytelling will have a host of benefits for your children and your family, helping your children master new language, ideas and emotions while building their confidence in communication. Storytelling can also create a safe, intimate, special time for being together.

Seven important benefits of home storytelling are:

- Language – a way of actively building vocabulary, comprehension and communication skills, not just by listening but by actively using language;
- Ideas – a way of engaging with ideas about the wider world beyond our own direct experience;
- Emotions – a way to explore empathy and emotion through putting ourselves in a character's shoes;
- Creativity – a way of building up the creative imagination of a child through the images and ideas of the stories themselves;
- Confidence – a way to help children become confident communicators through storytelling as they learn that their voice is valued by others and can be a pleasure to hear;

- Intimacy – a way to create a supportive and loving space for story sharing and story play;
- Values – a way to introduce and explore values through story.

Inside this volume you will find a set of 'World Stories' for reading, retelling and reflecting upon in the family. They are all 'traditional' meaning they have come from the spoken word tradition of storytelling. All will have been shared as spoken word and retold in various ways in families and communities around the globe. Such stories evolve with time as new tellers add their own ideas and twists to the tale, and are suited to spoken word telling: easy to remember and easy to retell.

They are here to share within your family in whatever way you choose: read them, tell them from memory, change them, re-enact them, discuss them, paint them, play with them and above all get your family to engage with them. You can find ideas for ways to do this in *Smith and Barron (2020) 147 Storytelling Games and Creative Activities for the Classroom.*

One simple way to teach your child to tell these stories is by using the Hear-Map-Step-Speak (HMSS):

- First read or tell the story to your children.
- Then have each draw a little map of the main events.
- After that practice 'stepping' through the story with a gesture and phrase for each step.
- Finally have a go at telling the story, using the map and gestures to aid memory.

For more details about HMSS and other aspects of the Storytelling Schools method see *Smith, Guillain and Barron (2020) The Storytelling Schools Method: Handbook for Teachers.*

This book is popular with parents who use storytelling at home. You might also have a look at the HMSS section on the Storytelling Schools YouTube channel.

These stories come from a collection of traditional stories for use in primary schools called *147 Stories for Primary School Children to Retell*. The main idea was to provide a set of tried and tested stories as a springboard for learning. Since then, the stories have travelled to schools around the globe, providing a tried and tested way of learning language, communication and creativity. In 2020/21 during COVID lockdown, for example, more than four million online lessons were downloaded which used these stories as the starting point.

I hope that you and your family enjoy exploring these stories together. You will then join the countless storytellers around the globe who have told and retold these tales over the centuries. May they continue to bring pleasure, learning and community to families around the globe.

Although the book is notionally for children aged 6–8 years, all of these tales can be adapted for a wide range of ages. Also, the content of traditional stories reflects the time and place in which the stories evolved. Some tales may include behaviour or ideas which are at odds with modern values, for example concerning attitudes to gender, marriage and human rights in general. Where this occurs the stories provide an opportunity for you as a parent to discuss and reflect on this with your child.

1. Lazy Jack

Here's a popular English classic. This one is comedy all the way so you can tell it like a stand-up comedian. Jack can be enthusiastic but a bit foolish, with his mum getting fed up with him. Then she can be delighted when it all turns out right!

Once, upon a time there was a boy whose name was Jack. He lived with his mother in a little cottage next to the village common. They were very poor. Jack's mother made a little money spinning wool and selling it, but Jack never helped at all. He did nothing but lie in the sun in the summer, and sit by the fire in the winter, warming his hands. So they called him Lazy Jack.

One day his mum got angry. She said, 'Jack, it's time you helped around the house. If you don't start working and helping then you'll have to leave. It's up to you. Off you go!'

'OK, Mum. I'll try!'

The next day he went over to the neighbour's farm and worked all day building a fence. Hammering and sawing all day. The farmer paid him a penny. On the way home Jack stopped at a lake. He didn't really understand about money. 'I wonder what this penny is for?' he thought. 'It would be good to skim on the water.'

So he skimmed the penny on the lake. It jumped three times and then disappeared under the water. 'Not bad!' he thought and went home.

'How did you get on today?' said his mum.

'I did well!' said Jack. 'I worked all day sawing and hammering, got paid a penny, then I skimmed the penny on the lake and it jumped three times! Busy day!' He grinned and waited for his mum to praise him, but she frowned, 'Jack, that's not the way to do it. You should have put it in your pocket and brought it home, not skimmed it on the lake!'

'OK, Mum,' he said. 'I'll try again tomorrow.'

The next day, Jack went out and got a job milking cows. All day he sat and pulled on the udders filling bowl after bowl with rich creamy milk. At the end of the day he was paid a jar of milk. Jack was walking home with the milk when he remembered what his mum had said. He took the milk and poured it all into his pocket. It went everywhere! None was left by the time he got home.

'How did you get on today?' asked his mum.

'I did well!' said Jack. 'I worked all day milking the cows, got a jar of milk, and then I did what you told me. I poured it into my pocket and walked home, and here I am. Busy day!' He grinned and waited for his mum to praise him, but she frowned, 'Jack, that's not the way to do it. You should have carried it on your head, not put it in your pocket.'

'OK, Mum,' he said. 'I'll try again tomorrow.'

The next day, Jack worked in a dairy helping make cream cheese. They paid him with a bowl of soft cheese. Jack was walking home with the cheese when he remembered what his mum had said. He took the cheese and put in on his head. It went into his hair and ran down his head and shoulders. None was left by the time he got home.

'How did you get on today?' asked his mum.

'I did well!' said Jack. 'I worked all day making cheese, got paid a bowl of cheese and then I did what you told me. I put the cheese on my head and walked home, and here I am. Busy day!' He grinned and waited for his mum to praise him, but she frowned, 'Jack, that's not the way to do it! You should have put it in a bag and carried it home, not put it on your head.'

'OK, Mum,' he said. 'I'll try again tomorrow.'

The next day, Jack worked in a bakery making bread, mixing the dough, putting it in tins and baking it in the oven. They paid him with a big strong cat. Jack was walking home with the cat in his arms when he remembered what his mum had said. He'd brought a paper bag specially, and so he tried to stuff the cat into the bag. It scratched and bit and ran off.

'How did you get on today?' asked his mum, back home.

'I did well!' said Jack. 'I worked all day making bread, got paid a big tom cat, and then I did what you told me. I put the cat in the bag but it didn't like it and ran away. Then I walked home, and here I am. Busy day!' He grinned and waited for his mum to praise him, but she frowned, 'Jack, that's not the way to do it! You should have tied a string around its neck and pulled it home on a lead, not put it in a bag.'

'OK, Mum,' he said. 'I'll try again tomorrow.'

The next day Jack worked for a butcher, chopping and cleaning and weighing the meat. They paid him a large piece of meat – a leg of lamb. Jack was walking home with the lamb when he remembered what his mum had said. He took the leg of lamb and tied it to a piece of string, then pulled it along the ground. Soon dogs followed him and ate all the meat. None was left by the time he got home.

'How did you get on today?' asked his mum, when he got home.

'I did well!' said Jack. 'I worked all day at the butcher's and got paid a leg of lamb. Then I did what you told me. I tied the meat with a piece of string and walked home. The dogs ate the meat, and now I'm home. Busy day!' He grinned and waited for his mum to praise him, but she frowned, 'Jack, that's not the way to do it! You should have carried it on your shoulders, not dragged it along the ground!'

'OK, Mum,' he said. 'I'll try again tomorrow.'

The next day Jack worked for a cattle farmer, looking after the cows, feeding them with straw and grain and cleaning their pens up. They paid him with a donkey.

Jack was walking home with the donkey when he remembered what his mum had said. He took the donkey and lifted it up onto his shoulders and tried to carry it home. He kept falling over and picking it up and doing his best to carry the donkey.

He was walking past the house of a rich man, and a rich man's daughter looked out of the window. She had never spoken since her mother died years before. The rich man had tried many cures but nothing had worked. Finally, he had promised that anyone who could make her speak would get twelve bags of gold. The rich man's daughter looked out the window, saw Jack trying to carry the donkey, and smiled. The smile became a grin. The grin became a snigger. The snigger became a laugh. 'Look, Dad!' she shouted. 'Look at that silly boy!'

The father was so happy. He walked out into the street and gave Jack a big hug! 'Well done!' he said. 'That was a brilliant idea what you did with the donkey!' Jack grinned. 'Thanks! It was my mum's idea really. She's very clever!'

Jack took his twelve bags of gold and walked home with them.

'How did you get on today?' asked his mum.

'Good,' said Jack. 'I worked all day for the cattle farmer. Got paid a donkey. Carried it on my shoulders like you told me, and got paid twelve bags of gold by the rich man for carrying it, and now I'm home. Busy day!'

'Well done, Jack!' said his mum and took the gold inside. And they were never hungry again.

And that's why it's always good to do what your mother tells you...

2. Cap of Rushes

This is another popular traditional English story. To tell it you need a good strong character for the father (foolish) and the daughter (patient). The image of losing her royal clothes and dressing in reeds is powerful. In the end I like the way the father repents and she forgives him. Put strong feeling into that final scene.

Once, a rich man had three daughters. The first was tall and greedy, the second short and jealous, and the third young and thoughtful. One evening the king sat them all down and said, 'Tell me daughters. How much do you love me?'

'As much as a king loves gold,' said the eldest and he rewarded her with a bag of gold. The second thought about how to get more than the first. 'As much as a queen loves diamonds,' she said and got a bag of diamonds.

The youngest thought about it for a while and then said, 'Father, I love you as much as food loves salt.'

The father frowned. Salt wasn't worth much, he thought. 'She insults you!' whispered the greedy daughter.

'She doesn't love you!' murmured the jealous daughter.

'Do you love me that little?' he shouted. 'After all I've done for you?' 'I love you as much as food loves salt,' she said firmly.

'How dare you!' he shouted. 'Get out of my house!'

There and then he pushed her out of the house. 'Never come back!' he shouted as she walked away, sobbing into the forest, with only the dress she was wearing on her back.

She walked and walked until she came to a marsh. She picked some reeds and plaited them into a hood and dress and hid her other dress inside a tree.

Soon she came to a grand house and knocked on the door. A butler answered. 'I am looking for a job,' she said.

'Go round the back!' he shouted, 'To the servants' entrance!'

At the back door the cook gave her a job scrubbing pans and cleaning the floor until her hands were red and raw. The cook asked her her name but she was silent.

'Why are you wearing a dress of rushes?' Again, no answer.

'Then we'll call you Cap of Rushes.'

In a house nearby, a prince was having three days of dancing and feasting so he could choose a wife. All the rich young girls were invited.

'Shall we watch them arrive?' said the servants to Cap of Rushes. 'No thanks,' she said. 'I have to clean the floor.'

When they were gone, Cap of Rushes slipped back into the forest, put on her lovely dress and went to the party. All night she danced with the prince.

The next morning the servants were chattering to Cap of Rushes. 'You should have seen the girl,' they said. 'She was lovely and had a fabulous dress. He danced with her all evening but nobody knows who she is!'

'Really!' said Cap of Rushes and smiled.

The second night the servants asked her to come and watch. 'No,' she said. 'I have to scrub the pans.'

When they had gone she slipped off again and put on her dress. She danced with the prince all night.

In the morning the servants said, 'Oh she's so lucky! He'll marry her for sure, but who is she??'

Cap of Rushes smiled.

On the third night the prince asked her to marry him and she accepted.

At the wedding feast her father was invited. Cap of Rushes wore a thick veil so he would not recognise her. She ordered that no salt be put in the food. The guests sat and chewed on the food but it tasted terrible. Her father sat there crying. From behind her veil she asked him why.

'I was a fool,' he said. 'I threw my daughter out even though now I see she loved me most of all. All I wish is to see her and beg her forgiveness.'

Cap of Rushes threw back her veil.

'Then your wish will come true. Here I am father and I love you still, you silly old man!'

From that day on, every time they put salt on their food, they remembered their love for one another.

3. The Marriage of Ganesh

This story from India is great for all sorts of teaching. First, it's a conflict between two brothers and is great for practising dialogue and character development. Secondly, one brother travels all the way round the world so you can use it to teach about any country you like. Third, it's all about the imagination and how much we can learn from stories. Get the two characters clear and the story will work well. Practise telling the punch line for maximum impact. Traditionally, the story is used to show that there are always many valid points of view for any issue. Two obvious talking points are the role of the princesses in the story and the wider issue of polygamy.

Elephant-headed Ganesh, the God of Success, was sitting in his library. In two of his hands he was holding a book and was thoughtfully turning the pages. In his other two hands he was carefully cutting and eating a mango.

Suddenly his brother Kartikeya burst into the room. 'Brother, brother!' he said, excitedly, 'I've got something to tell you.'

'Oh yes?' said Ganesh thoughtfully.' And what would that be?'

'I think it's time I got married. I'm old enough now and I've decided who to marry. You know those two princesses from the temple, Siddhi and Buddhi? I want to marry them. What do you think of that, brother?'

Ganesh stroked his long trunk and smirked. 'I'm older than you,' he said. 'Maybe I should marry them.'

Kartikeya stamped his foot and shook his head. 'But it's my idea!' 'And now it's my idea too,' said Ganesh.

'Maybe we should fight for it? The winner gets the girls,' said Kartikeya.

'I'm not that stupid!' purred Ganesh. 'You're the God of War! That's like me saying, 'Let's decide it with a quiz.' You'd have no chance!'

'Well, how about a race around the world?' asked Kartikeya enthusiastically. 'I love races.' Ganesh thought about it, then said carefully, 'Do you mean that I can travel around the world in my own way, in any way I wish, and if I get around the world before you then I win the girls?'

'Yes, that's what I said!' snapped his brother. 'Agreed,' said Ganesh.

'Great! One, two, three – GO!'

Kartikeya ran out of the library, out of the palace and up the Himalayan mountains. At the top he stopped and looked around. There was snow at his feet and eagles circling below him. He saw the tracks of a snow leopard on the edge of the forest but there was no sign of his brother!

He slid down the mountains and was soon in the forests of China, running past panthers, tigers, even the odd panda or two.

He ran and he ran until he reached the rice fields and on through field after field until he reached the sea.

Then he swam from island to island, past dolphin, whale and shark.

He reached America and ran deep through the Amazon forest and up to the buffalo plains, running north with the buffalo, occasionally stopping to hear their stories, until again he was swimming in the sea.

Onwards, through blocks of ice, he swam to the frozen plains, passed polar bear and seal, over the top of the world and down the Russian Steppes beyond, until finally he was back where he started.

He looked for Ganesh and found him in the library. He was reading a book and eating a mango.

'Welcome back,' said Ganesh. 'Where have you been? I've been waiting for you, so you can be at my wedding.'

Kartikeya was astounded. 'What? How do I know you really did travel around the world? You don't look as if you've moved from that chair!'

'I could ask you the same thing,' said Ganesh. 'How do I know you went round the world?' 'Hmm. So tell me, brother. If you went round the world, tell me what it was like,' asked Kartikeya. 'Where did you go first?'

'It was very cold. There was snow on the ground. I saw eagles and snow leopards, and loads of big woolly yaks.'

'Hmm. And what then?'

'Through the Chinese rainforests, full of so many animals: tigers, pandas, snakes – you name it!'

Kartikeya's face fell. 'And then?' 'Rice fields – all the way to the sea.'

Ganesh described his journey to his brother in great detail, noting all the things that Kartikeya remembered and more. In the end Kartikeya was persuaded. 'OK, brother,' Kartikeya said. 'You've won. Marry them then!'

And so Ganesh married the two princesses. After the wedding, Kartikeya came over to his brother. 'Brother, did you really travel the world? I'm still not really sure about that.' 'Well, yes and no,' said Ganesh. 'You travelled round the world your way and I travelled round the world my way.'

'How do you mean?' asked Kartikeya.

'While you were running and swimming, I was reading. I read book after book about every country on the journey. As I read I saw them all in my imagination. In that way, I travelled around the world.'

'Hmm...' said Kartikeya. 'Isn't that cheating?'

What do you think?

4. Baba Yaga's Black Geese

Here's a Russian tale, this time with a heroic heroine. It's a witch story, so make her as horrible and nasty as possible. When the action starts, make sure the audience feels the danger. When the magic starts try and convey the wonder. I learned this one from storyteller Adam Guillain.

Once upon a time, on the edge of a forest in a little cottage there lived a family: a mother, a father, a daughter and a little baby boy. The daughter's name was Olga and the baby was called Sergei. Every morning when the parents went off to work in the fields, the mother would say to Olga, 'Don't forget to stay in the garden. Never go out into the forest, or the witch, Baba Yaga, will get you and eat you and your little brother up.'

One day Olga was feeling a bit bored looking after the baby all by herself so she picked him up and walked out of the garden, through the gate and off into a field by the forest. She laid her brother down in the grass and started picking flowers for her mum. Just then three huge black geese flew over the field, picked up Sergei in their beaks and carried him off into the forest. Olga chased after them.

She ran and she ran and she ran until she came to a fish lying on the path by a stream. 'Olga, Olga, Olga!' called the silver fish. 'Help me!' Olga threw the fish into the stream. It popped its head out of the water and swam towards Olga with a shell in its mouth. 'You have helped me and now I will help you,' it said. 'Take this shell and if you need help throw it over your shoulder. I will come and help.' Olga took the shell and continued along the path.

She ran and she ran and she ran until she came to a squirrel caught in a trap.

'Olga, Olga, Olga!' called the squirrel. 'Help me!' Olga pulled the squirrel free from the trap. It scurried off up a tree and came back with an acorn in its claws. 'You have helped me and now I will help you,' it said. 'Take this acorn and if you need help throw it over your shoulder. I will come and help.' Olga took the acorn and continued along the path.

She ran and she ran and she ran until she came to a mouse that couldn't get into his hole because it was blocked by a pile of earth. 'Olga, Olga, Olga!' called the mouse. 'Help me!'

Olga moved the pile of earth and the mouse scurried off into its nest. Moments later he came back with a tiny stone. 'You have helped me and now I will help you,' it said. 'Take this stone and if you need help throw it over your shoulder. I will come and help.' Olga took the stone and continued along the path.

She ran and she ran and she ran until she came to Baba Yaga's house. Peering in through the window she saw the old witch asleep in her rocking chair. Her face was green and grey, her nose was long and twisted and her lips were thin and mean. Sergei was playing happily on the floor with a pile of bones. Olga tiptoed in through the door, picked up Sergei, and, as quick as a flash, was out of the door running for her life. Baba Yaga woke and saw the baby was gone. 'Who's taken my dinner?' she screamed and went chasing after Olga.

Olga ran and she ran and she ran, but the witch was close behind ... just about to grab her when she remembered the shell. Olga threw the shell over her shoulder and a great lake appeared between her and the witch. Baba Yaga stopped, bent down and drank up all of the lake. Then she chased after Olga again.

Olga ran and she ran and she ran, but the witch was close behind ... just about to grab her when she remembered the nut. Olga took it from her pocket and threw it over her shoulder. A forest sprang up behind her, so thick that the witch could not get through. Baba Yaga opened her mouth and ate up the forest, then chased after Olga again.

Olga ran and she ran and she ran, but the witch was close behind ... just about to grab her when she remembered the stone, took it out of her pocket and threw it over her shoulder. It turned into a huge mountain. Baba Yaga stopped and stared at the mountain. She couldn't eat it; she couldn't climb it; she couldn't go round it and so she went back to her house.

Olga ran home, shut the gate behind her and put little Sergei to sleep in his crib. He was fast asleep when their parents came home from the fields.

'How was your day?' asked the mum. 'Fine,' said Olga.

And that was the end of that...

5. Three Brothers and the Polar Bear

This is a riddle story originally from India but reset in the Arctic. The story sets up a discussion at the end: a good story to lead into argument and persuasive writing. It's important to convey the showing off quality of the brothers as they demonstrate their skills, and then something of the horror of being hunted by the polar bear.

Once upon a time in the land of ice, seals hunted fish, polar bears hunted seals and man hunted polar bears (although sometimes man was hunted too, by the polar bears).

In the land of ice lived three brothers. When they finished school each travelled to study in their chosen subject.

The first brother studied skeletons and how to piece them back together from a pile of bones. He became a bone expert.

The second studied a kind of magic where he could conjure up blood, flesh and fur to reveal a dead corpse around a skeleton. He became a corpse maker.

The third brother studied the dark art of bringing life back to the dead. He became a life bringer.

One day, soon after they finished their training, the three brothers were walking home across the ice when they saw a pile of bones.

'Look what I can do!' said the first brother. He started to snap the bones together and had soon re-made the complete skeleton of a polar bear.

'Pretty good,' said the second brother. 'Look what I can do!'

The second brother poured a magic potion onto the bones, whispered a spell, and conjured organs, meat, veins, flesh and fur, leaving the body of a dead polar bear lying on the ice.

'Pretty good,' said the third brother, 'but look what I can do!'

The third brother closed his eyes and chanted the life-giving chant, then bent down and breathed life into the polar bear. The polar bear's heart started beating, its lungs started moving, and then its eyes opened.

Then its mouth opened and it ROARED! It was hungry and saw breakfast.

The brothers ran across the ice.

The bear caught one brother and tore him limb from limb. The second died from the first bite, and the third was eaten bit by bit, scream by scream, till there was only his sealskin boots left in a pool of blood.

What a sad end for the brothers... after all that study!

But here's my question for you:
Who was most to blame for their deaths?

6. Three Dolls

Here is a wonderful story explaining how stories help us learn language. It's also a great way to teach the class riddles and have them teach you some too. Maybe before you tell the story you can ask them to collect riddles from home and see what they bring. Riddles make great mini-stories. In this story the character of the teacher and daughter is important. Slow down when she explains about the dolls, so suspense can build. I developed this story from a lovely version by David Novak.

Once upon a time, when riddles were still the judge of character, there was a teacher. He was a good teacher, a fine teacher. When he walked down the street children would get excited and say, 'That's our teacher. He knows lots and lots of things!'

Parents would speak to the teacher with respect and almost reverence. 'We're so lucky to have such a clever teacher!'

They'd even bow sometimes to him in the street. Can you tell that this is an old, old story?

In class he would talk, talk, talk, and the children would listen, listen, listen.

Some students remembered what they heard and wrote it down in the exams – they were considered good students. Some students couldn't remember what he said. It went in one ear and out the other – they were considered bad students.

One day he said to his class, 'Tomorrow is riddle day. Bring riddles to ask me.

See if you can beat me. If there's one I can't guess then you can choose what we do in class for the rest of the term.'

So the children went home and they collected their riddles and they brought them back to class the next day.

'Teacher, teacher, what is it that has two hands and a face but no feet?' 'Why a clock, of course.'

'What runs all day yet stays in one place?' 'A river.'

'What has a head, a foot and four legs?' 'A bed.'

The teacher was pretty good and guessed all the riddles until the storyteller's daughter stood up with three dolls in her hands.

She asked, 'What is the difference between these three dolls?' The teacher couldn't tell the difference. They all looked the same.

He sent the children out to play, saying that he would have the answer upon their return. First he asked the smartest student in the school to see if she could see any difference between the three dolls. She measured them, smelt them, examined them very closely and said, 'They're all the same.'

Then the teacher asked the most foolish student in the school the same question and he said, 'Of course they are different, look, this one is an aeroplane!' and the foolish child took one of the dolls and started to zoom it around the classroom. '...and the other two are in love!' and he made the two dolls kiss!

The children came in from play and the teacher said to the storyteller's daughter, 'There is no difference that I can see. So if you can show me a difference, you win.'

'The difference is on the inside,' she told him. 'Come here and I'll show you.'

He bent down toward the doll and looked. Quickly she plucked a long white hair from his beard.

'OW!' he said. 'Why did you do that?' 'Wait and see.'

Taking the hair she pushed it into the first doll's ear till it came out through the other ear, out the other side.

'This is what you call a bad student,' she said, 'because what goes in one ear comes out the other.'

She plucked a second hair and poked it into the ear of the second doll. It stayed in and didn't come out the other side.

'This is what you call a good student,' she said, 'because what goes in the ear stays in the mind.'

She took a third hair for the third doll. This time it went in one ear and out the mouth. 'But teacher, this is the best doll. This is a storytelling doll. In this one it goes in through the ear and then out the mouth. And look! It comes out differently, with a curl!'

'And why is that the best doll?' asked the teacher.

'Because that's what we need for life, teacher. Listening's fine but we need to be able to take the things we've heard and talk about them, explain them, storytell them. Everyone needs that to do well in the world.'

'So,' said the teacher smiling, 'You've won. What is your wish?' 'I want us all to learn to be storytellers.'

So the teacher taught his students to tell stories.

And that's how the first storytelling school began.

7. The Lighthouse Keeper and the Selkie

A selkie is a woman who is sometimes a seal and sometimes a woman. Britain's seal-rich coast is full of stories about selkies and their contacts with humans. Here's one example from Scotland. Emphasise the loneliness of the keeper, the wonder of seeing the seal women, his happiness during marriage and then his sorrow at the end.

Once there was an island. A small rock in the sea. On the island was a lighthouse. Nothing else, just a lighthouse.

The lighthouse keeper lived there alone. Every night he lit the lamp so that the ships would stay clear of the rocks. In winter the seas were rough and no boat could reach the lighthouse. In summer it was warm and quiet. He was quite happy in this peaceful life, but sometimes he felt lonely and wished that he had a wife to keep him company.

One night he was sitting on a rock fishing in the sea, when he saw seven seals come ashore on the beach. As he watched in the moonlight they slipped off their sealskins and stood up as lovely young women. They were changelings! They were selkies – seals in the sea and women on land. He watched as they laughed and danced and played together, singing and clapping.

As they played he sneaked over to one of the skins and took it back to the lighthouse, locked it in a wooden chest then returned to the beach.

As the sun rose the selkies slipped on their skins and slid back into the sea. One woman stayed behind, looking for her skin.

The lighthouse keeper walked towards her with a blanket. 'It's OK,' he said quietly. 'I won't hurt you. Let me help.'

She let him cover her with a blanket and lead her to the lighthouse. She stayed there with him, living as his wife. She didn't cook or clean. She just spent her days staring out at the sea with tears in her eyes. When she saw seals she would call out to them in a strange language and they would call back.

Sometimes she'd sing to the sea:

> *Take me home, rolling sea,*
> *To the place I belong*
> *Take me home, rolling sea,*
> *Take me home.*

The lighthouse keeper was so happy to have such a beautiful wife. He loved to sit by her in the evening telling her stories and singing her songs.

Time passed and she gave birth to three lovely children. He was so happy.

Then one day the eldest was playing in the lighthouse store when he found a key. He looked and looked till he found the chest it fitted and inside was a smooth sleek pelt.

He took it to his mother. Her eyes lit up.

'Come, children!' she said and walked with the three children down to the sea. 'Hold my hands!' she said as she slipped on the sealskin.

The keeper saw them on the beach and walked down to join them but when he arrived all he could see was a mother seal with three baby seals swimming out from the rock.

He never saw his family again.

8. Death in a Nutshell

Here's another great story about death and dying. This time the focus is on why things must die and what would happen if they didn't: lots of talking points and personal relevance. The son is the key character who cannot stand the idea of his mother dying. Get into that role and the story will flow easily. You can tell it in a tender way, with as much crazy comedy as you like in the middle. Activist storyteller, Eric Maddern, has written a lovely picture book about this story.

Once there was a long straight beach of stone shingles. Behind the beach was a tiny cottage where a mother lived with her only son. The father, a fisherman, had been killed in a storm soon after the boy was born and his mother had raised him alone, living off the food from a small plot of land behind the cottage, and occasional work mending the fishermen's nets. Soon after the boy's eighteenth birthday his mother fell ill and took to her bed. He made her soup, but she wouldn't take any.

'I'm tired,' she said. 'I feel like my life will end soon.'

'Don't talk like that,' said the boy. 'You've many good years ahead of you. I'll take care of you.'

'No, son,' she said. 'I'm tired. I think my time is coming.'

The boy stepped out of the cottage for a breath of fresh air and walked down to the beach. Just then he saw Death walking along the beach toward the cottage with a grim grin on his face. He knew that Death had come for his mother.

'No!' he shouted, 'I won't let her die!'

He picked up a piece of driftwood, rushed at Death and started to pound him with the piece of wood. He pounded Death smaller and smaller until he was the size of a nut then, picking up two halves of a walnut shell from the beach he stuffed Death inside, tied the nut closed and threw it with all his might, out into the sea.

Pleased with himself, he went back to his mother's bedside.

'I'm feeling better,' she said. 'Can you make me some chicken soup?'

'Sure!' said the boy happily and went out to the chicken coop with his chopper. He picked out a fat chicken and took it squawking to the chopping block. Stretching out the neck he chopped through it with the axe, and was about to start collecting the blood when the chicken head flew up off the ground and stuck itself back on the chicken body. The boy looked on in disbelief as the chicken started squawking and clucking again.

'I must be dreaming,' he thought and chopped off the head a second time. Immediately the head snapped back on again.

'Strange,' he thought. 'I'll try another chicken.'

But the same thing happened again. The chickens just would not die.

'I'll make some vegetable soup,' he thought and pulled up some onions and carrots but the moment he laid them on the kitchen table they flew through the air, out of the window and planted themselves back into the earth where they had been pulled.

The boy went down to the village to buy some food, but there was no meat in the butcher's and no vegetables at the grocer's. There was nothing to buy and nothing to eat! Everyone was talking about how nothing would die, so how could they live!

Perplexed, he went home and told his mother what had happened.

She gave him a piercing look. 'What have you done, son? Tell your old mum!'

So he explained about meeting Death and how he had tied him up in a nutshell and thrown him away, to save her life.

The old lady shook her head.

'That's no good,' she said. 'Things need to die so we can live. There'll be no food now, but also people need to die when they get old. Without death our bodies would fall apart but we'd still be alive, suffering in terrible pain. There's no life without death, my boy. Now off you go and set Death free!'

Easier said than done. The boy went back to the beach and looked out to sea but there was no sign of the nut. Then he felt the tide push something against his toes. He looked down and there was the nut.

'She's right,' he thought. 'There can be no life without death. When her time comes I must accept it.'

He opened the nut and Death jumped out, no worse for wear. He tipped his hat to the boy and walked up the path to his cottage. The boy sighed and followed Death inside to his mother's bed.

He held his mother's hand as she slept into a deep sleep and, with a relieved smile on her face, she died.

Her son spoke at the funeral. He said there could be no death without life and no life without death. His mother had led a good and kind life and he was proud to be her son. He loved her and missed her, but death comes to us all and this was her turn. After the funeral he sat outside the cottage and began to grieve.

9. The Fox and the Healer

Here's a mysterious shamanic-type tale from North America. I like it because it is not really clear what is going on and it gives the audience lots to think and talk about. At the same time it is set in snow and ice with all sorts of possibilities for imagination and descriptive work. Good for using all the senses. Hear Hugh Lupton's brilliant version on Tales of Wisdom and Wonder *from Barefoot Books.*

Once there was a village of tipi tents, camped on the edge of a plain. In one of the tents a young girl was sick, coughing and sweating with fever. Her parents sent for the old healer and she came right away, hobbling on her walking stick into the light of the tipi fire. The old lady knelt down and pressed her ear to the little girl's chest, and stayed there for a while.

'What are you doing?' said the mother.

'Shhhh!' said the woman. 'Patience!'

'What can you hear?' asked the father a little later.

'I hear the sound of a fox. She is running over snow, but she is sick. She is looking for a warm place but can find neither food nor shelter. I can hear the sound of her footsteps. They are too slow.'

The girl's father was a hunter. He said, 'Shall I go and find the fox and bring it back here?' 'Yes,' she said. 'That will help a lot!'

The girl's father pulled on his furs and set off into the night. After a while, by the moonlight, he found some fox tracks in the snow and started to follow, running through the deep thick drifts.

He ran and he ran and he ran as the old lady listened in the tent.

'Good!' she said. 'Now I can hear the footsteps of the hunter. He is running fast while the fox is slow. I can hear all that!'

The father ran and he ran till a day later he caught sight of the fox. The fox turned and stared at him.

Back in the tent the old lady smiled.

'Good! I can hear them both now, together. She has seen him. Soon he will help her.'

That night the hunter built a fire and took some rest while the fox watched from a distance. Back in the tipi the old lady said, 'Good! Now I can hear the flames of the fire. She will have a fever now to burn away the sickness.'

And the girl's face burned all through the night.

The next morning the fox was too tired to move and the hunter picked her up.

Back in the tent the old lady said, 'Now she is frightened. Now her heart is beating fast. Soon they will be home!'

The next morning they were home and the hunter laid the fox down next to his daughter. The old lady made a bed for the fox in the furs by the fire.

'Get me some meat!' she said and fed it to the fox, who ate hungrily. Then fox and daughter slept for a whole day.

When the fox woke up she jumped up and ran out of the tent. 'Shall I follow?'

asked the father.

'No!' said the woman. 'No need now!'

The daughter stood up and walked towards the tent flap. She was well again. She stared out at the fox as it trotted away, fit and healthy,

The father looked at the old woman.

'Tell me,' he said, 'how did the fox cure the girl? How did the girl cure the fox?' That's what he asked, but the old woman gave no answer.

What do you think?

10. Jack and the Dancing Trees

There's something about trees getting up and going for a dance that I find quite lovely. There are all sorts of artistic possibilities with dance and 3D art here. The story also notes the summer solstice, which is good to be reminded of. It's also a fine fable about greed and nongreed with a lovely love interest. Enjoy! You can find a version on the web in verbatim dialect told by Scottish storyteller, Stanley Robinson.

Once there was a shepherd boy called Jack. He worked for a rich farmer looking after his sheep as they grazed through the long summer months. Jack loved being outdoors, watching the birds fly and the salmon leap. He loved the oak woodland on the farmer's land, with its huge ancient trees. The farmer was rich and greedy and paid Jack almost nothing for his work, but Jack didn't mind. He was content.

One day Jack's mother brought him lunch of bread and cheese to the field where he was watching his sheep.

'Jack,' she said, 'last night I had a dream. I saw all the trees in this wood uproot themselves. They walked down to the river and started to dance. I saw sparkling jewels in the places where they had been rooted. Do you know what this means?'

'You had a nice dream?' said Jack.

'No, Jack! Don't you know the legend? They say that once every seventy years, on midsummer's night, all the trees of this forest go down to the river to dance and mate, and that in the holes they leave behind there is treasure. Once they've finished the dancing they go back and reroot themselves but, on that night, if you're quick, you can find treasure there.'

'Really!' said Jack, wide-eyed.

'Yes!' said Jack's mum. 'So listen, Jack – tonight if you wait and watch, once the trees have gone off to their dancing, jump into one of the root holes and take one or two jewels. Not too many or you'll never get out. Just one or two. And take this rope. You'll need it to get out.'

She handed him a rope which he put in his pocket and she went off home. Jack lay down on the grass and made up a song:

> *Once in a while, the trees go down,*
> *Down to the river to dance.*
> *Once in a while, the trees go down,*
> *And then I'll take my chance.*

As Jack was singing the farmer came over to Jack, checking up on his work.

'What are you doing, Jack?' asked the farmer. 'What's that about the trees dancing?' 'I'm thinking,' said Jack.

'I don't pay you to think!' snapped the farmer. 'What are you thinking about?'

'Tonight's the night, once in seventy years, when the trees go down to the river to dance. I'm thinking about that and if I can find some treasure tonight.'

'Really?' said the farmer. 'How interesting!'

Now Jack was very fond of Mary, who worked in the farmer's kitchen. A while later she came rushing over to Jack, flustered.

'Jack, Jack!' she said, 'I heard the farmer talking to his wife. He's coming tonight for the tree treasure, and he's taken a knife. I think he means you harm. He was saying the treasure belongs to him and not to you! Be careful!'

Jack gave her a hug and said he would be fine, she shouldn't worry.

As the sun set Jack was hiding behind a bush watching the trees. Once the sun was gone there was a creaking and a groaning and he watched the trees pull up their roots and walk off down to the river. Then he heard the sound of knocking and drumming as the trees began to play their music and dance their dance.

Once the trees were gone, Jack went over and stared into the hole left by a giant oak. It was full of jewels! He was just about to jump down when a voice shouted:

'Oi! Jack! You keep away from that hole! That treasure is for me!'

It was the farmer with a knife in one hand and a big sack in another.

Jack backed away and the farmer jumped into the hole, and started stuffing gold and jewels into the sack. Jack noticed that every time he picked up a jewel, the hole got a bit deeper. He watched the farmer going deeper and deeper into the ground as the sack filled with jewels till he was just a tiny speck in the distance.

Jack went to another tree hole and jumped in. 'Just a few jewels,' he said to himself.

He picked up three shining jewels, a diamond, an emerald and a ruby, and put them in his pocket. Jack looked up and saw that the hole was now three times as deep as he was tall. How could he get out?

Just then Mary appeared.

'Throw me the rope, Jack, and you can climb out.'

He threw up the rope and she tied it to a rock. As Jack climbed out he realised that the music had stopped and there was the sound of root steps coming up the hill.

'That was quick!' he thought. 'What about the farmer?'

They looked down the hole and he was almost out of sight, deep in the ground, still stuffing jewels into the sack.

'Come out!' shouted Jack. 'They're coming back!'

But the farmer only had eyes for the jewels. Moments later the oak stepped back into its hole.

The farmer was never seen again.

And as for Jack, he sold the jewels and bought a lovely little cottage next to the oak woods and lived there happily with Mary and his mum. Seventy years later, when Jack was 86, on midsummer's night, Jack's grandson went up to the woods with his granddad and waited...

But that's another story...

11. Little Burnt Face

Here's a First Nation story about honesty and integrity with a love interest, linked up with magic warrior powers. It's a sort of golden apple story but this time it works out well! You can play the start for comedy, the middle for tension, and the end for happiness. There are many versions on the web and in print. One good variant is in the Anthology of Children's Literature by Johnson and Scott.

Once there was a warrior called Strong Wind. He knew powerful magic and could make himself invisible at will. He could walk amongst his enemies and hear their plans. He could hunt and kill without being seen. Enemies were defeated without seeing him. In this way he became famous.

Many women wished to marry such a powerful man, and went to his tent to ask. Each one was given a test: they were taken down to the river by his sister and made to wait for a while, then she would ask:

'Here he comes along the road. Can you see him?' 'Oh yes!' they'd answer, although they could not. 'And how does he pull his sledge along?'

Now they had to guess.

One said with rope, another said with string, another said with leather straps.

No one ever guessed right. The sister knew they were liars, and sent them off home.

In a nearby village the chief had three daughters. As children the youngest was gentle of heart and beautiful of face. The other daughters were so jealous that they stole her clothes and jewellery and cut off her hair. When she still looked beautiful they took burning coals and pressed them into her face, and told her father she had done it herself. She was then known as Little Burnt Face.

One day the eldest daughter went to offer to marry Strong Wind. The sister took her down to the river.

'Do you see him?' asked his sister.
'Oh, yes!' she said.
'Then how does he pull his sledge?'
'Hmm... with a wooden handle?'
'No!' said the sister and sent her home.

Next the middle daughter tried her luck.

'Do you see him?' asked his sister.
'Oh, yes!' she said.
'Then how does he pull his sledge?'
'Hmm ... with leather rope?'
'No!' said the sister and sent her home.

Then Little Burnt Face went to the tent, dressed in her rags.

'I would like to marry Strong Wind,' she said.
'Come,' said his sister.
They waited for a while down by the river.
'Can you see him?' asked the sister.
'No,' said Little Burnt Face, sadly.

Strong Wind heard her truthfulness and her kind heart, and revealed himself to her.

'Oh yes!' she said laughing. 'There he is!'

'So how does he pull his sledge?'

'It is wonderful! He pulls it with a rainbow!' and she smiled at the wonder of the sight.

'Yes! Now what is the bowstring made of?'

'Wow! It's made from the stars of the sky!'

'Yes!' said the sister.

She bathed the girl in the river, gave her fine new clothes and rubbed a healing balm on her burnt face so the scars were gone. She gave her necklaces and earrings and bracelets and sent her to Strong Wind's tent.

They were married and together practised magic for the good of all.

As for the sisters... if you were Strong Wind, what would you do with them?

12. The Monk and the Thieves

Here's a trick tale from Chile: you might tell it with puzzlement and suspense as your audience tries to make sense of what is going on.
Get the clever, tricky character of the monk and the gullible nature of the cattleman. Play out the ending and the foolish nastiness of the thieves.

Once a cattleman was walking along the path towards home when he heard a sound coming from a big brown sack.

'Let me out!' it shouted. 'Help!'

He untied the sack and out hopped a monk. 'Thank you, my son,' the monk said. 'I am saved!' 'What were you doing in there?'

'You'll never believe it. Four thieves told me about how they had stolen a pile of gold. I told them stealing was wrong and they wanted to give it to me. Then, when I refused – as monks should never own things, especially stolen things – they said they would kill me and put me in the sack. They're going to throw me in the river!'

'Well, I could have the gold,' said the cattleman. 'Let's swap clothes, sew me in the sack and when they come back I'll tell them.'

'Fine,' said the monk and sewed him up inside. Minutes later the thieves came back.

'Let me out and I'll take all your gold!' the cattleman shouted. The thieves shrugged and threw him in the river.

The cattleman was just about to drown when someone pulled the bag onto dry land and let him out. It was the monk.

'I'm not a monk,' he said. 'I was pretending to be a monk to collect money, but when I saw the thieves' gold I tried to steal it and they decided to kill me. But give me my clothes back and I'll get their gold – half for me and half for you! Just lend me your cattle for half an hour, that's all.'

The cattleman wasn't sure but in the end he agreed.

The monk went to the thieves followed by all the cows, and started singing.

'Aren't you dead?' they asked.

'No. I am alive and very rich. At the bottom of the river is a fairy kingdom. I went there and they rescued me and gave me all these cattle as a present. It's lovely down there.'

The thieves looked at the cows.

'Do you think they'd give us some if we went there?'

'Definitely,' said the monk.

'So please throw us in the river!'

'OK!'

The monk tied them in four sacks, loaded them on a boat and let it float off downriver, then collected up the thieves' gold and split it 50/50. The cattleman was rich!

13. The Story Bag

This is a much-told story about stories needing to be told and what happens if they get bottled up inside. I can't imagine why storytellers like it! It's a great theme to discuss and allows for lots of innovation – which stories would you find in your bag? Daniel Morden tells a brilliant version of this story if you ever get a chance to hear him. Practise doing different voices coming from the bag to bring the moment alive, and find a character feel for the servant as a loving and wise man. Build up suspense for the final scene – what will happen to the servant?

There once lived a very rich family. They had only one child, a boy, who loved to have stories told to him. Whenever he met a new person, he would say, 'Tell me a story. I'd love a new story.' Every time he heard a new story he'd store it away in a small bag, which he kept on his belt. Soon the bag was packed tight and he had to push the new ones in hard to fit them in. He kept it tightly tied so no stories would escape.

Time passed, the boy grew into a man, met a woman, and planned to get married. Everyone in that rich house was involved in planning the wedding and getting ready to welcome the bride to her new home.

In the house there was a faithful, old servant who had known the boy since he was a child. One evening before the wedding, he was working in the kitchen when he heard a strange voice coming from the corner of the room even though there was nobody else in the kitchen. He followed the sound and realised it was coming from a bag hanging on the kitchen wall. It was the story bag hanging on the wall, long forgotten by the young master of the house.

'Listen, everyone,' said a voice. 'The boy's wedding is to take place tomorrow. He has kept us this long while stuffed in this bag, never letting us out at all! Now's a good time to pay him back and get our revenge!'

'I agree,' said another voice. 'How about this? Why don't I change into bright red berries on the path to his bride's house? He'll eat a few and they'll be poison. That way he'll die and it serves him right for keeping us locked up like this.'

'Yes, and after that, if he's still alive,' squeaked a third voice, 'I shall become a clear spring by the path with a cup to drink from. He'll fill the cup, drink, and then I will poison him.'

A fourth voice than broke in, 'Good idea! And if he's still alive I'll become a red hot chunk of metal. When he gets off his horse at his bride's house he'll step on me and burn his feet terribly, then die a slow and horrible death. That'll sort him out!'

A fifth voice whispered, 'If that fails too, I shall become a poisonous snake, hide in the bed, and bite them both when they are asleep.'

The next day was the day of the wedding and the servant was ready to help his master. Early that morning, the groom came out of the house and mounted his horse. The servant came running out and grabbed the horse's bridle and asked to be allowed to lead the horse, but the young master said, 'You have other work to do. You had better stay behind.' 'But I must lead the horse today,' the servant said. 'I don't care what happens, but I insist that I take the bridle.'

He refused to listen to anyone and finally the master, surprised at the old man's obstinacy, allowed him to lead the horse to the bride's home.

All the family set off following the young master's horse in a long joyful procession. Berries grew all along the hedgerow. They looked sweet and lovely.

'Wait!' the bridegroom called out. 'Stop the horse and pick me some of those berries.' The servant kept leading the horse as if he didn't hear. Then he said, 'Oh, those berries. You can find them anywhere. I can pick some for you later.' And he gave the horse a good crack of the whip.

The groom was surprised at this but said nothing.

Next they came to a spring with a lovely shining cup next to it.

'Bring me some of that water!' the bridegroom said to the servant. 'I have been thirsty for some time.'

But, again, the servant refused his order. 'Once we get into the shade of those trees, your thirst will soon disappear,' he said, and urged the horse on.

'Do what you are told, man!' shouted the groom, but the servant just ignored him. The bridegroom was surprised at this unusual behaviour.

Soon they reached the bride's home. There, already gathered in the yard, was a large crowd of people. The servant led the horse into the compound and stopped it in the centre of the yard. As the groom stepped down from his horse, the servant pushed him over out of the way of the burning metal. Immediately the metal disappeared.

The bridegroom blushed with shame at his clumsy fall. However, he didn't want to scold his servant in front of all the people so he kept silent and entered the bride's house.

They were married in the house, and then the couple began their journey to the groom's home. They arrived surrounded by the family and danced and drank till late into the night.

Finally they went to their bedroom. The servant hid behind the curtain in the bedroom with a sword and waited. As soon as the bride and bridegroom were in bed, the servant jumped out from behind the curtain and onto the bed. He pushed them out of the way and turned over the mattress revealing a huge black snake under the bed. He killed it with one cut of his sword.

'How did you know?' asked the young master.

'Well, I was in the kitchen last night and I heard the stories in your bag talking...'

He told the whole story from start to finish and the master rewarded him with one hundred gold coins.

Soon the young master became a father. He made sure to tell his children all of the stories that he had heard as a child, opening the neck of his story bag so his stories were free to come and go as they pleased.

So the master and his family and all their stories lived happily ever after.

14. How a Boy Learned to be Wise

I love this little known story about coming of age and learning to live with others. It's from Uganda so you can set it in Africa if you like. The theme of the child who disappoints his parents is a great one to work with. Almost everyone can identify with this. Here the hare is the wise and trusted friend. Get in touch with your inner wise person and your sulky child when you tell it. Also it's good to explain about potters before you start.

Once upon a time, in a little village by the deep green forest, there lived a potter with his wife and one child, a little baby boy. The boy never played with his parents or with other children. He never laughed or sang. Mostly he just sat by himself, alone, and did very little. This made his parents worried.

One day the potter spoke to his wife:

'Wife,' he said, 'maybe our son will become a fool and maybe he will become wise, but let's not worry about it. Let's just wait and see what happens.'

The boy heard all this and he thought about it all night. In the morning he walked off into the forest to think some more. All day he wandered about, singing a song like this:

> *Foolish or wise, foolish or wise, what's the one for me?*
> *Foolish or wise, foolish or wise, what am I going to be?*
> *Thinking I am foolish fills me up with fear*
> *But how can I learn to be wise? I've really no idea.*

He walked and walked until he came to a little clearing and sat down for a rest, still singing his song: *Foolish or wise, foolish or wise...*

A lion appeared from the trees and walked towards him.

'I heard your song. What are you doing here?' said the lion.

'I am sad because I don't know if I am wise or a fool,' he said. 'Is that what you are thinking about?' said the lion.

'Yes,' answered the boy, 'I think about it all the time.'

'Then you are a fool,' said the lion. 'Wise men think about things that benefit others.' The lion walked back to the forest.

The boy went back to his song:

> *Foolish or wise, foolish or wise, what's the one for me?*
> *Foolish or wise, foolish or wise, what am I going to be?*
> *Thinking I am foolish fills me up with fear*
> *But how can I learn to be wise? I've really no idea.*

An antelope came into the clearing and stopped to stare at the boy.

'I heard your song. What are you doing here?' it asked.

'I am sad,' said the boy, 'because I do not know whether I am wise or a fool.'

'When do you eat?' asked the antelope.

'I eat when my mother cooks for me,' said the boy.

'And when do you thank her?' said the antelope.

'Never,' said the boy. 'I just eat!'

'Then you are a fool,' said the antelope. 'Wise men say thank you!' The antelope ambled off back to the forest.

The boy felt sadder and went back to his song: *Foolish or wise, foolish or wise...*

Just then a leopard came up and looked at him.

'I heard your song. What are you doing here?' he asked.

'I am very miserable,' answered the boy. 'I don't know if I am a wise man or a fool.'

'Do you have good friends in your village?' asked the leopard.

'Not really,' said the boy. 'I don't get on well with the other boys. They don't like me.'

'Then you are a fool,' said the leopard. 'Wise men make friends and earn respect.'

The leopard walked back to the forest.

The boy went back to his song: *Foolish or wise, foolish or wise...*

Just then an elephant came out into the clearing.

'I heard your song. What the matter?'

'I am sad,' said the boy. 'I don't know if I am a wise man or a fool.' 'What job do you do?' asked the elephant.

'I don't have a job,' said the boy.

'Then you are a fool,' said the elephant. 'All wise men have work to do.'

The elephant went back to the forest and the boy went back to his singing, sobbing as he sang.

Foolish or wise, foolish or wise...

As he sang tears rolled down his cheek. A hare came out of the forest.

'My little brother, do not cry so! Tell me your trouble,' said the hare. 'I am sad because I am a fool,' he said. 'All the animals say so.'

The hare said: 'It is true that you are a fool. It is true that the wise think of others, are thankful and friendly and work hard. All animals work hard, and you should do the same. Why waste your time doing nothing?'

'Maybe I shall be a potter like my father,' said the boy.

'If you are to be a potter,' said the hare, 'then be the best in the country. Wise men do the best they can.'

The boy went home. When he saw his mother he said:
'Thank you for all the food and care you have given me,' and she smiled.

He said to his father, 'I would like to be a potter. Will you teach me how?' and the father smiled.

The boy worked hard and studied hard and became a great potter. Everything he made was beautiful and sold for a good price.

Sometimes he would go to the edge of the forest and sing his song:

> *Foolish or wise, foolish or wise, what's the one for me?*
> *Foolish or wise, foolish or wise, what am I going to be?*
> *Thinking I am a little bit wise makes me feel quite good.*
> *I'd rather be wise than foolish, I really think I should.*

The little hare would come running down the forest path, and the two friends would spend a long day together. The boy would tell all his heart to the hare, and the hare always listened and gave good advice.

And his parents were happy and proud of their son till the end of their days.

15. Persephone

Here's our first Greek myth. If the class don't know about these myths then start by explaining a bit about the gods and their qualities:

Zeus – King of the Gods; Hades – God of Death; Demeter – Goddess of Life; and Persephone – daughter of Demeter. Too many new and unfamiliar names can lead to confusion with an audience so find an activity that gets them familiar with their names and attributes. This story is hugely popular. It's generally easy to identify with the fear of separation from parents and so children can connect well with the story. Of course there can also be the wish to separate from parents, so you can tell the story that way too if you like. It also provides a delightful way of explaining the seasons.

Demeter was Goddess of Life. Everything grew and lived on earth because of her.

Demeter had a daughter called Persephone, who she loved more than anything.

One day Persephone was picking poppies in a field of corn when Hades, God of Death, appeared in his chariot. He picked her up and took her down under the earth to his home.

When Demeter couldn't find her daughter she was sad. She looked everywhere but couldn't find Persephone, and became so sad that she stopped smiling, stopped speaking, and stopped making life on earth.

The world became cold. Nothing would grow. Nothing could be born. Everything began to die.

Down under the earth, Persephone was sad too and missed her mother. Hades wanted her to stay and marry him but she said no and refused to eat or drink anything. After a few days she became hungry and ate just six seeds of a pomegranate fruit.

Up above the earth Zeus, King of the Gods, was worried. The earth grew colder and colder and nothing could grow. He asked Demeter to make life again but she shook her head, 'Not without my daughter!'

Zeus went to talk to Hades.
'You must let her go!' he said, 'Or everything on earth will die! You cannot make her stay unless she has eaten food from this place.'

Hades smiled.
'She has eaten six seeds from a pomegranate! So now she will stay.'

Zeus thought about it for a while.
'If she has eaten six seeds then she will stay with you for six months of the year. And for six months she will live above earth with her mother.'

So from that time to this, Persephone spends half the year under the earth. During this time Demeter is sad and the world grows cold, with nothing growing. This time we call winter. For the other half, Persephone returns to her mother, who happily makes new life for earth. The world grows warm and everything can grow again. This time we call summer.

16. The Wooden Horse

This must be one of the most famous trick tales in the world.
It a good action-thriller story if you can spin it out a bit.

Long ago the kingdom of Troy was at war with Greece. A Trojan prince, Paris, had run away with the beautiful Greek queen, Helen. She was a married woman. When her husband found out he rounded up all the Greek kings and declared war on Troy. They would win back his wife and punish this insult to all Greeks.

A great fleet of Greek ships set sail for Troy, but when they arrived there they realised that they would have a long wait. Troy was surrounded by a high stone wall that no army could overcome by attacking.

So instead the Greeks laid siege to the city, letting nothing in or out for ten long years.

Ten years later the Trojans were still living fairly comfortably inside. They had their own stores of food and a water supply for drinking, and could wait for another ten years if need be.

But the Greek kings couldn't wait another ten years. They wanted to get home to their kingdoms and families.

Then one of the Greek kings, clever Odysseus, made a plan.

They made a huge wooden horse as high as ten men and mounted it on a cart with six giant wheels, so that it could be moved around. Then all of their ships set sail and left the shores of Troy, leaving only the wooden horse behind.

From the walls of Troy the Trojans were delighted, 'We've won! We've won!' they called as they ran down to the beach to celebrate, dancing and singing around the wooden horse which the Greeks had left behind.

The king of Troy looked carefully at the huge wooden horse.

'This is an offering to the gods,' he said. 'We will take it into our temple in the city and honour the gods with it too, and thank them for helping us win this war.'

So they tied long ropes to the wooden horse and one hundred men pulled it through the city gates and into the temple courtyard to the cheers of the Trojans inside the city.

That night, while the Trojans were drinking and dancing, the Greek ships sailed back in darkness to the shores of Troy. Not a single light was lit, so they would not be discovered. Then they sat and watched and waited...

Inside Troy a small secret door opened in the belly of the wooden horse and a rope snaked down to the ground. Odysseus silently slid down the rope and another ten men followed, with swords and daggers ready for fighting.

They hardly needed them. All of the city was busy celebrating and there was nobody to stop them as they crept through the streets towards the city gate. They spied out the four guards and at the same moment slit their throats without a sound being heard.

Then, as quietly as possible, they pushed open the great gates of the city.

Moments later the armies of Greece stormed through with swords drawn and blazing torches ready to burn and destroy. It was all over quickly. Soldiers rushed out of their homes; many were killed before they even found their swords. The palace of the king was unguarded and easily taken.

Soon the whole of the city was brimming with Trojans running for their lives.

Within a few hours the city was taken. The Greeks had won the war by the trick of the wooden horse.

17. Half a Blanket

I really like the way traditional stories often teach about respect and care for elders. In cultures where youth is valued over age these provide great talking points. Here's a sharp little tale about that from Scotland, with lots of role-play options in the tale, replaying family narratives. Try and bring alive the depressed father, the ailing grandfather and the loving daughter.

Once there was a woodcutter. He lived with his wife, daughter and father in a little house on the edge of a forest. Every day he went off to work chopping wood in the forest, selling the wood in the town and bringing home whatever food he could buy for the family.

Sometimes there was enough food, but sometimes they all went hungry. This made him sad and frustrated. He hated to see his family suffering and felt like he was a failure.

His father had been a woodcutter like him and in the past had gone to the forest with him every day. Then they had collected more wood and more food, but as the old man got older his joints became stiff and his back became bent. It was all he could do to walk from his bed to his chair. He couldn't even help around the house. The old man felt bad about this. He spent more time by the fire chatting with his granddaughter, who loved spending time with her kind old granddad.

Time passed and the two men started to argue about one thing or another. The father felt criticised. The woodcutter felt taken for granted. The father felt unwanted. The woodcutter felt resentful.

One evening the whole thing blew up and the father said, 'Fine! If I'm not wanted here then I'll go and live somewhere else!' and walked off towards the door.

'That suits me just fine!' snapped the woodcutter.

It was midnight. There was snow on the ground and the nearest neighbour was half a mile away.

The woodcutter just sat there scowling as his father opened the door.

'Daughter!' he called out angrily. 'Go and get Granddad a blanket and give it to him, to keep him warm on the road.'

The girl looked carefully at the woodcutter and said, 'No Dad, I think we should only give him half a blanket.'

The woodcutter was surprised. He knew the girl was fond of her granddad. 'Why, Daughter?'

The girl looked her father straight in the eyes. 'I'll keep the other half to give you when you get old and have to leave.'

The two men stared at the girl, and then the woodcutter walked over to his father and led him back to the fire.

'Sorry, Dad!' he said. 'Please stay with us.'

18. Fruit of Love

I was taught this First Nation story by storyteller Michael Moran, when I was looking for a story on the theme of forgiveness. It's simple and can be told in many ways. The main thing is to stoke up the anger of the argument, the stubbornness of the person walking away (either wife or husband, up to you!), and then the tenderness of the ending. It can be retold between the first two friends if that's more suitable.

In the beginning when the world was new, First Man and First Woman were having their first argument. Whatever it was about, they shouted and got more and more angry. I wonder what they were arguing about? Finally First Woman walked off across the desert, her nose in the air, grumbling to herself.

'How dare he say that to me! How dare he! I'll never speak to him again! He's horrible. I hate him!'

First Man began to feel worried. 'I was angry,' he thought, 'but now I'll never see her again. Oh no! What have I done?'

He prayed up to the sky to the God of Love. 'Bring her back to me, please! I love her.'

The God of Love was watching the whole thing. He thought, 'She'll never come back while her nose is sticking up in the air like that. I'll have to get that nose down.'

And so the God of Love covered the desert in a blanket of lush green leaves. 'That ought to get her nose down!' he said.

But it didn't work. She didn't even notice. She carried on grumbling, with her nose in the air.

'I'll have to try harder,' thought the God of Love and created a sea of tiny white flowers blooming on top of the green leaves.

First Woman still didn't notice. She kept on striding away from her husband and grumbling. Her nose stayed stuck up in the air.

The God of Love thought about it some more. 'This is harder than I thought,' he said, and created a carpet of wonderful sweet-smelling red fruits.

Maybe it was the colour. Maybe it was the smell. First woman stopped and looked down. She bent down and picked one, and tasted it, biting it in half. The fruit tasted sweet.

She looked at the half that remained. It was in the shape of a heart with a sweet tender inside.

'Hmm ... I suppose I do love my husband even though he's a fool,' she thought. She picked up a handful of heart-shaped fruits and took them back to her husband. And that's how the first strawberries came into the world.

19. One Wish

Here's an example of the popular 'one wish' story retold with a football interest. That makes it a bit more interesting for the football fans in your class. Obviously, just change the name of the place, river and the local team. When it has been learned the tellers can add any team they like. It's good practice for punchline telling.

O nce, in the city of Oxford, there lived a man. He was a good man, a kind man, and a happy man, but three things made him sad.

First, he was a keen football fan and supported Oxford United. Unfortunately they kept losing. Second, his old mother had lost her sight and was finding life very difficult. And third, he had been married for ten years but had no children, and his wife really wanted children badly. One day the man was walking down by the River Thames, right by a pub called *The Isis*, when he saw a fish flapping on the bank. He bent down, gently picked the fish up and returned it to the river. The fish popped its head up out of the water.

'Thank you,' it said. 'And as you've been kind to me, I shall be kind to you. I will give you one wish, but choose wisely – you only have one.'

The man thought, 'I could wish for Oxford United to do well... or I could wish for my mother to have her eyesight back, which would make her really happy... or I could wish that my wife and I finally have the son we've longed for.'

He thought very hard then had an idea. He looked down to the fish and spoke. 'I wish that one day my mother will see my son score the winning goal for Oxford United in the FA Cup Final.'

From that day his mother's sight started getting better until she could see again. A year later his wife gave birth to a little baby boy, and today he's playing centre forward for Oxford United's youth team. In a few years' time, who knows what will happen!

Snip snap.
That's the end of that.

20. Birth of Athena

*I like the way this story gives a positive spin to having a headache.
Or to put it another way, sometimes learning things can be painful!
Explain in advance that Athena was Goddess of Wisdom, talk a bit
about what that means, and then tell this story about how she was
born. It can be fun to make up new birth tales with the class.
Also explain about Zeus, unless you have already done so.*

Soon after Zeus became King of the Gods he got married to his first wife, Metis.

It wasn't long before she was pregnant. At first he was happy at the thought of being a dad, but then someone whispered in his ear, 'The child in your wife's womb will be greater and wiser than you.'

Zeus did not like the sound of that. There was a history of trouble between fathers and sons in his family!

'I am the King of the Gods,' he thought. 'No one should be greater and wiser than me.' So he came up with a plan to stop his child being born.

'Wife,' he said, 'let's play a game. Let's see who can turn themselves into the biggest creature.'

She turned herself into an elephant and he into a giraffe. 'It's a draw,' he said. 'I am taller but you are heavier.' 'Now, let's see who can be the fastest creature.'

Metis became a greyhound and Zeus became a falcon. 'Still a draw,' he said.

'Let's see who can be the smallest.'

Metis turned herself into a fly and hovered in front of him. Zeus grabbed the fly and swallowed it.

'That's the end of that child!' he thought with a smile.

But... a few months later Zeus's head started to ache. The pain got worse and worse until it felt as if a spike was pressing hard into his brain from the inside of his skull. There was a voice too, inside his throbbing head.

'Let me out! Let me out!' it cried.

Zeus wasn't sure what to do, but the pain got worse and worse until he just had to do something.

He summoned Hephaestus, the blacksmith, who took out a hammer and chisel and cracked open Zeus's skull.

Out leapt a goddess with a roar, a helmet on her head and a spear in her hand. She was Athena, the Goddess of Wisdom.

And that is how Wisdom came into the world. So, if you ever find yourself with a really bad headache, or some other kind of ache, don't worry, it might just be Wisdom trying to come out.

21. The Lode Stone

Here's a lovely little tale about paying attention and noticing what is important. You can make the main character a bit wild and obsessive.

Once upon a time there was a pebbled beach ten miles long. Legend said that on that beach there was one stone that had the power to turn iron into gold – the Lode Stone.

A man decided that he would find the Lode Stone. He started at one end of the beach, picked up the first stone and held it against the iron buckle of his belt. When nothing happened, he tossed it over his shoulder and tried another one. He held the next stone against his belt and waited and when nothing happened, he threw it over his shoulder again. He touched, waited and threw, touched, waited and threw again and again and again and again.

In this way he moved across the beach. A day passed, then a week, then a month and then a whole year.

As time passed, the man became quicker and quicker with his actions. He touched, waited and threw, touched, waited and threw, faster and faster, keen to get to the end of the beach. After five years he had combed almost the entire beach without discovering that stone.

One day, a boy eating an ice-cream asked him what he was doing.

'I am searching for the Lode Stone,' he told the boy. 'The stone that has the power to turn iron into gold. I pick up each stone, touch it against my iron belt and wait. If nothing happens I throw the stone over my shoulder.'

The boy looked at the man's belt. 'But your buckle is gold,' he said.

The man looked down and, sure enough, his buckle was gold. Sometime over the last five years the man had stopped looking properly and along the way must have actually had his hands on the Lode Stone.

He let out a long, long sigh and trudged all the way back to his house to find another old belt. Then he made his way to the other end of the beach and started again, this time paying much more attention.

Many years later, a young girl playing in a rock-pool on that beach saw an old man with wobbly knees and a crooked back picking up stones and holding them to his belt.

'Your belt!' she called. 'It's so beautiful! Is the buckle gold?' The old man sighed... 'Here we go again!'

22. The Scorpion and the Frog

Here's a very popular little Asian fable that pops up all over the place. It is told by the main protagonist in the movie The Shawshank Redemption as a fable for how life can be. It can be about the way we can all sow the seeds of our own destruction just by 'being ourselves'. Get two clear voices for the two animals and create tension as the frog tries to decide what to do.

Once there was a scorpion, a creature with a deadly sting in his tail. One day he decided to travel to visit his relatives across the river. When he got to the riverbank he saw a frog.

'Brother Frog!' he called. 'Let me ride on your back across the river. I can't swim and I need to visit relatives on the other side.'

'Do you think I'm stupid?' croaked the frog. 'I know you scorpions. If I let you get near me then you'll sting me and kill me!'

'Why would I do that?' asked the scorpion. 'I need a ride over the river and if I sting you then you will die of the poison, but I will die from drowning. So of course I won't sting you.'

'Alright then, Brother Scorpion,' the frog agreed reluctantly. 'Climb on my back and I'll give you a ride.'

Halfway across the river the scorpion stung the frog on his back. The frog started to sink as the poison filled his body.

'Why did you do that, Scorpion? You promised not to!' cried the frog.

'I am a scorpion. It's in my nature to sting!' answered the scorpion, as the waters closed over his head and the two creatures sank to their deaths.

23. Three Wishes

I first heard this story from the inimitable TUUP at the Crick Crack Club in London, who told the 1001 Nights version. He was very funny! Here is the sausage version; there are many such tales featuring foolish wishes, including an old English version featuring a black pudding collected by Joseph Jacobs.

The story is all about foolishness and impatience so you have to evoke the foolish character in a funny, crazy way!

Once there was a fisherman. One day he was walking by the river when he came upon a silver fish, flapping on the riverbank. He felt sorry for the fish and threw it back into the river.

The fish popped its head out of the river and spoke.

'You have helped me so I will help you. You and your wife may have three wishes. Wish for anything you want and wish well.'

The fisherman went off home to tell his wife the good news. When he got home she was standing at the cottage door frowning.

'No fish for me to cook?' she said. 'What have you been doing all day? I am hungry and we have nothing to eat.'

'Wife, I have good news. I helped a fish and now we can have three wishes!'

'Mmmm,' she said, smiling. 'That's good. What I would like now is a lovely big sausage!' Just then a long fat sausage appeared in her hand, cooked and ready to eat!

She smiled and prepared to take a bite.

'You foolish woman!' he shouted. 'You have wasted our wish on a sausage when we could have had anything. You don't deserve to eat it. I wish it was stuck to your nose!'

Just then the sausage stuck to her nose.

She pulled and pulled but it would not come off. He tried but she just wailed.

'It won't come off,' she wailed. 'It is stuck there forever. What shall we do with the last wish?'

The fisherman began thinking about all the things he wanted. A new house, money, power...

... But then he looked at his wife sobbing with the sausage on her nose, and felt sorry for her.

'Wife,' he said, 'You can't go through life with a sausage on your nose. I wish the sausage were gone!'

And just like that the sausage disappeared.

'Oh well,' said the fisherman. 'If I ever get three wishes again I will be more careful.' 'Me too,' said his wife.

If you had three wishes, what would you choose?

24. The Blind Man and the Hunter

This is a much-loved and commonly told story from West Africa. There is a lovely text version in McCall Smith's The Girl Who Married a Lion. *Here there are two main characters to develop – the wise brother and the arrogant hunter who learns to be more humble.*
There are lots of chances to describe an imagined African jungle and lots of talking points about world affairs and what to do.

Once there was a forest and in the forest was a village and in that village there were huts woven from branch and earth. In one of these huts there lived a blind man. The man was greatly respected in the village. It was said that even though he could not see with his eyes, he could see with his ears. People came to him with their problems and found his listening satisfying. He shared his hut with his sister, who looked after their home and looked after a small piece of land where they grew vegetables and kept a few goats for milk.

They lived happily together.

In another hut there lived a hunter. He was a skilled hunter, proud of his ability with the bow and trap. He considered himself the best hunter in the village and, after a few cups of palm wine, he'd sing a little song to himself:

> **A-hunting I will go.**
> **A-hunting I will go.**
> **There's nothing so fine**
> **As a man in his prime.**
> **A-hunting I will go.**

One morning he noticed the blind man's sister working on her land and fell in love with her quiet simple beauty. He courted her and within a month they were married. Sister and brother moved in with the hunter.

Every day the hunter would go out to the forest, trapping and tracking, and every evening he'd come back with his kill and hand it over to his wife for cooking. He'd lie in his hammock and sing himself his song:

A-hunting I will go...

He'd sing himself to sleep till the food was ready. He never once thanked his wife for her work in the home.

One day the family was eating supper. The hunter was chatting away about his adventures in the forest when the blind brother interrupted, 'Let me go hunting with you tomorrow. I can help you.'

The hunter laughed. 'What! You? What possible use could a blind man be to me?' He went back to his story.

The blind man shrugged and went back to his supper.

The next day the blind man asked again. 'Let me go hunting with you tomorrow. I can help.'

'Look, I've told you. You can't help. I am fine. I go hunting. I bring the food. She cooks it and you eat it. That's it. You can't come.'

Every day for one hundred days the brother asked to go hunting, but was always dismissed as being of no use until finally the hunter relented. 'OK brother, tomorrow you can come. Just once. Then maybe you'll stop bothering me.'

The next day the two men set off into the forest. For a while the hunter sang his hunting song as they walked, the blind man followed him easily along the path without help. After a while the blind man said, 'Shhh! Careful! There's a lion with her cubs nearby, over there that way.'

The hunter stopped singing. 'How do you know?' he asked doubtfully.

'I can hear them playing.'

The hunter listened but could only hear the wind in the trees. He peeped around the corner and sure enough, there was a lioness with a handful of suckling cubs, lying in the sun. Very dangerous! The two men tiptoed away and the hunter went back to singing again:

> *A-hunting I will go...*

After a while the brother said, 'Shhh! Careful! There's a mamba snake on the branch above your head. Move away slowly or he may strike.'

The hunter looked up and saw the snake poised ready to strike. He moved away quickly. 'How did you know?' he asked, impressed.

'I smelled its scent,' answered the brother.

The hunter went back to his song, but soon the brother stopped for a third time. 'There's a family of elephants down by the river. Should we go the other way?'

The hunter listened but couldn't hear the river, let alone the elephants. They walked for a good ten minutes before coming to the river where a family of elephants were playing and washing. Now the hunter was really impressed.

'Maybe a blind man can be of use after all,' he thought, but did not say it.

They came to a clearing and the hunter showed the brother how to set a bird trap. The hunter set one trap and the blind man another, and then they went on their way. Then they went hunting with bow and arrow. The brother listened out for prey and the hunter watched. The blind man was really useful, the hunter realised.

That evening at supper the hunter said, 'Brother, come hunting with me tomorrow. Let's see what we have caught in our traps.'

The brother nodded and smiled.

The next morning they came to the clearing where they had set the traps. There was a bird in each. In the hunter's trap was a plump brown bird and in the blind man's trap a bird about the same size but covered in the most beautiful feathers, all the colours of the rainbow.

The hunter liked the coloured bird more. He felt a little jealous. 'Well done!' he said to the brother as he took the birds out. 'You have caught a bird on your first try. Here, take it.' He handed him the brown bird.

The blind man nodded and said nothing.

The hunter took the rainbow bird as his kill and together they walked home.

Somehow the hunter felt uneasy all the way home. As they approached the village he stopped. 'Brother,' he said, 'you are said to be wise so tell me. Why is there so much trouble in the world?'

The brother replied quietly, 'It is because of people like you, who do what they should not!'

The hunter flushed with shame. 'I am sorry, brother. I was selfish. I thought you wouldn't know or wouldn't care but it was wrong. Here – take the rainbow bird.'

The brother nodded and they exchanged birds.

They walked for a while longer and the hunter stopped again. 'So tell me. So many people take what is not theirs. Is there any hope for the world then?'

'Oh, yes!' he said smiling. 'There is hope. Because there are people like you who can admit their mistakes and learn from them.'

The next day they went off into the forest together:

> *A-hunting we will go.*
> *A-hunting we will go.*
> *There's nothing so fine*
> *As men in their prime.*
> *A-hunting we will go.*

25. The Birth of Osiris

This is our first creation myth. Find a voice to tell it in that conveys the enormity of creating everything! Maybe explain at the beginning that it is from Ancient Egypt and tells the story of Ra the Sun God and his children, Osiris and Isis. Get them used to these names before you start. There is a love interest here and how you handle it depends partly on the maturity of your class and partly on how confident you are. Creation by alphabet can be fun if you want to play it with your class. These kinds of stories have a huge and different atmosphere that children love to experience and create. Try using a drum in parts of the story for atmosphere. I like the treatment of these and other stories in Morley's Egyptian Myths.

In the beginning there was only water. Water in all directions, into infinity. Nothing else. Then the creator spoke his own name from inside the water. 'I am Ra.'

He rose up above the water, a blazing sun disk, and looked down on it. He began to name the world he would make.

He said, 'Earth!' and there was earth.
He said, 'Sky!' and there was sky.
He said, 'Mountain!' and there was mountain.
He said, 'Forest!' and there was forest.
He said, 'Desert!' and there was desert.

Next he named trees and bushes, flowers and grasses.

Then he named all the creatures of the earth – ant, bear, cat, dog, elephant, fox, giraffe, horse, iguana, jaguar, koala, lion, mouse, newt … he named them all.

Ra looked down on the earth and saw the animals playing and feeding, mothers feeding their young. He smiled and tears of joy fell from his eye.

Then he saw death and tears of pain fell from his other eye.

Those tears dropped from his eyes down into the ground and mixed with soil to become humans – humans made from the tears of the Sun God. Tears of joy and tears of pain. That is why we all have both joy and pain inside us.

Time passed. The Sky looked down at the Earth and the Earth looked up at the Sky. Each gazed at the other and liked what they saw. Sky admired Earth's mountains and valleys. Earth admired Sky's white clouds and dark twinkling night. They were in love. So Sky came down and wrapped herself around Earth.

Ra was watching and was jealous. 'No!' he commanded. 'You will not be married! Why should you be together when I am alone? Wind – push them apart, and keep them apart!'

Wind came between them and blew, pushed Sky up away from Earth, up so only the tips of Sky and Earth were still touching out on the horizon.

Soon Sky's belly began to swell. She was going to have babies.

Ra saw this and was furious. 'I am the creator!' he yelled. 'Not you! You will not give birth in any day of any year!'

Sky grew heavier and heavier with her babies but could not give birth. She moaned and groaned. Thunder roared and lightning flashed. 'Help! Someone, help!' she cried.

The God of Wisdom, Thoth, heard her cries and made a plan. He challenged the Moon to a game of chess.

'Listen,' said Thoth, 'let's play for something to make it interesting. Every time you win I'll give you some of my wisdom. And every time I win you give me some of your moonlight. Deal?'

'Deal!' said the Moon, and they started to play.

They played game after game, Thoth winning easily until he had enough light for five new days. Then he slipped those new days in between the old and new year. Ra knew nothing about the new days, and so his curse did not apply.

In each of those five days Sky puffed and pushed and gave birth to her five children. Among them was Osiris, who was to become ruler of the world, and Isis, who would become his queen.

26. Prometheus

This is another lovely creation myth, this time from Ancient Greece. I like the quality in this one of imagining physically moulding clay into men and women before giving them life. Get some modelling clay for a follow- up activity! A nice gory ending of unbearable torture – that's the joy of the Greeks!

When the world was new, Prometheus was given the job of starting life on earth. He lived in a high walled garden with a workshop where he made all sorts of creatures, keeping them all inside the high walls.

He made trees and flowers, bushes and grasses, fish and birds, lions and leopards, cats and cougars. On and on he worked making life after life and letting it out into the garden to see how each plant and animal would fit with the others. As the garden filled with amazing creatures he began to love them as if they were his children.

'They are good. They are beautiful,' he thought, 'but who will look after them once I have let them out into the world? Who will be their protector?'

One night he had an idea.

He took some river clay, mixed it with that-which-gives-life, and began to work.

He moulded a head, with two eyes, two ears, a nose and a mouth. He moulded a neck, shoulders and two arms, each with a five-fingered hand on the end. He moulded a chest and a belly. He moulded hips and legs, knees and ankles, and two five-toed feet.

In this way he created something that looked rather like the gods themselves.

When he'd finished he made another, and another, all through the night until the table was covered in a crowd of what looked like gods and goddesses. When they were finished he waited, and when the first rays of sun came up over the garden wall, the creatures came to life. Lungs filled with air. Hearts pumped blood around their veins. Their eyes opened and they climbed down from the table and walked out into the garden.

'Yes!' thought Prometheus. 'Now there are creatures that can protect and look after the life I have made. These humans are a little like gods. They can look after the earth and its life.'

He opened the doors of his garden and all the life he had made rushed out and into the empty world, which was soon covered with forests and jungles, plains and deserts – all filled with the life he had made and we humans with the job to protect it all.

Prometheus watched over his creatures out in the world, and soon noticed that humans were a little cold in winter. They needed something to keep them warm or they would die.

He sneaked up to Mount Olympus and took some of the gods' fire down to earth. He showed the humans how to use it to cook and keep warm.

But Zeus looked down from Olympus and was angry. 'How could Prometheus steal from us, the gods!' he thundered. 'For this he will be punished!'

They chained Prometheus to a cliff over the sea. Every morning an eagle would come and eat out his liver, slowly, bite by bite, agony by agony. Every night his liver would grow back again.

This was his punishment for bringing us fire.

27. The Eagle Who Thought He Was a Chicken

Here's a lighter tale after those heavy myths – a First Nation story about learning who you are. Some schools change it to 'The Red Kite Who Thought He Was a Chicken' so it can be connected to local fauna. You can play this for comedy as the powerful bird acts like a chicken, and then for celebration as he learns what he can really do. May we all follow in the story's wingbeats!

Once... there was a farmer. One day he was walking through a forest when he heard two gunshots up ahead on the path. A few minutes later he came to the bodies of two huge golden eagles lying on the ground, both stone cold dead.

'What a pity,' he thought, 'to kill such beautiful birds! They help keep down the numbers of rats and mice and rabbits and do little harm to us humans. They are the kings of the sky. Who would do such a thing?'

He looked up and saw an eagle's nest above his head in the highest branches of a tall pine. 'I wonder...' he thought.

Carefully he climbed up the tree and looked into the nest. There were two eagle eggs there, still warm. He slipped them into his pocket and climbed down.

Back at the farm, he wondered how to take care of them. He slipped the eggs under a hen who was hatching a clutch of her own eggs, and waited to see what would happen.

The eggs all hatched and the eaglets were accepted as part of the mother hen's family, one brother and one sister. She treated them as her children and they thought she was their mother. They learned how to live like chickens – how to cluck and scratch in the dirt, eat seeds and grubs, and how to hide when eagles flew overhead.

Time passed and the eaglets grew. Soon they were bigger than the other chicks. Their beaks were longer, their wings wider and their claws sharper. Still they continued clucking and pecking and scratching in the soil, running for cover when an eagle flew by.

One day, as the sun was going down, the brother eagle heard the sound of a huge owl hooting from the tree above the farmyard, except the owl seemed to be laughing. 'Hoot, Hoot, ha, ha, ha, hoot, hoot!'

'What are you laughing at?' asked the brother.

'I'm laughing because you are an eagle, but you walk and talk like a chicken!' 'No, I'm not!' shouted the brother, annoyed. 'I am a chicken.'

'Really?' said the owl. 'Then why are you so big? Why is your beak so long?' 'I'm an unusual chicken, that's all.'

The owl swooped down and landed next to the brother. 'Jump on my back and I'll prove it to you.'

The brother jumped on the owl's back. The owl took off and soon was flying high above the earth.

'I don't like it up here!' shouted the frightened brother. 'I might fall! Put me down! Take me back!'

'Sorry about this,' said the owl, 'but you'll thank me later!'

The owl turned upside down in the air and the brother fell off his back and started to plummet down towards earth.

'Heeeeelp!' he cried as he fell.

'The owl dived down through the air next to the falling bird, shouting, 'Open your wings! Open your wings!'

The brother opened his long brown wings and in a moment, he stopped falling and started to climb through the air, with the owl laughing next to him.

'You see!' the owl hooted. 'You are an eagle! You can fly!'

The next day the brother went to his sister. 'Jump on my back!' he said. 'I want to show you something.'

Soon brother and sister were circling above the chicken coop. Proud eagles. They felt like king and queen of the sky.

'Thank you, owl,' they called, 'for showing us who we really are.'

28. How Butterflies Came to Be

*This is another First Nation tale, this time about joy and beauty. Tell it
with tenderness. Find the things you love and put them in the story,
then get your class to do the same.*

In the beginning the Creator made all things: birds and bees, fish and fowl, plants
and porcupines, horses and humans. He made it all, then had a long sleep.

When he woke up he went for a walk to see how his creatures were getting on.

Fish were swimming, birds were flying, snakes were slithering. It all seemed to
be going to plan, till he came to a human village.

He noticed the children playing, laughing, singing and was pleased, but then
he saw their parents working and worrying about themselves and their families.
They had no joy, only hard work and worry.

'That's not right,' he thought. 'But what shall I do?'

He went off to the wise woman of the forest and asked her advice. She was
sitting in her hut smoking a pipe.

'The parents are all so serious!' he said. 'They have no joy, just duty! That wasn't
my plan. I made the world so they will have joy.'

'So,' she said, 'you have to make something to give them a little joy. Take the
best things from what you have made, the things that give you most joy, and mix
them together into something new. See what happens.'

He went out into the world and collected his favourite things:

Moonlight shining on the water
A flower's delicate petals
Pollen from a flower
The pattern of a snakeskin...

He collected them all and then mixed them all up in a bag, breathed in the breath of life, and out came...

Butterflies. Beautiful butterflies of every colour in the rainbow, delicate and beautiful.

As he watched they flew into the village. The children laughed and chased them around the streets.

Then the parents looked up, just for a moment from their work and worry, to see what was going on.

Each time they saw a butterfly they smiled, just for a moment before going back to work. And that's why, when you see butterflies, just for a moment, you find yourself smiling.

29. The Shepherd's Dream

*This mysterious Irish story allows the audience to puzzle and try to make
sense of its meanings. It takes us into the world of dreams where one thing
can stand for another. Tell it with wonder. I like Crossley-Holland's telling
in* Folktales of the British Isles. *You can also hear Hugh Lupton tell the
story on his* Tales of Wisdom and Wonder *CD.*

Once there were two shepherds who lay down to rest under a tree while their
sheep grazed the long green grass of the field. The shepherds had a lovely
view down over the field, over a sparkling stream and a bed of long golden reeds.
The sun shone down and all was well.

They smiled and sang a little song:

> **Life is a mystery.**
> **It's very hard to see**
> **What is real and what is true,**
> **What is me and what is you.**

Then the older shepherd puffed on his pipe and admired the view, while the
younger shepherd fell into a deep sleep.

Then something started crawling out of the young man's mouth. The elder
watched in amazement. It was a butterfly! How could that be?

The butterfly hopped out of the mouth, crawled down the young man's chin, neck
and belly and down onto the path. It fluttered down the path through the field

towards the stream. The old shepherd followed behind it, trying to make sense of what he was seeing.

At the stream there were some stepping stones over the river and the butterfly hopped from one to the next till it got to the other side, with the old shepherd close behind.

Next, it followed the path through a clump of bulrushes and out into a green field. The old shepherd watched as it flew to a bleached white horse's skull in the centre of the field.

He watched the butterfly fly into the eye-socket of the skull and disappear. He waited and a while later if flew out of the mouth and back towards him, over the field, through the rushes, over the stepping stones and up the path back to the young shepherd. There it crawled up his chin and disappeared back into the young man's mouth.

Moments later the young shepherd woke up. 'I've just had the most amazing dream!' he said. 'I dreamed I was walking down a road lined with tall green trees. I walked till I came to the ocean, and there I started flying, out over the sea from island to island, till I came to a new land where the trees where tall and thin and golden. I travelled through the forest of giant trees until I came to a white palace. I went inside but it was empty. Nothing there at all. So I came back home, through the forest of giant trees, over the ocean, island to island, then up the road surrounded by a green, green forest. Then I got home and woke up. What does it mean?'

'I'll show you,' said the elder shepherd.

He led the young shepherd down the pathway that led through the long green grass. 'In your dream, this was the road through the green forest,' he told him.

He pointed to the stream and stepping stones. 'This was the ocean and the islands.'

He led the young shepherd through the clump of bulrushes. 'And this was the giant forest,' he said and then pointed out the skull. 'And that was the palace.'

'This is amazing!' exclaimed the young shepherd. 'But what do you think it means?' 'I don't know,' said the elder shepherd. 'But it must be something wonderful.'

They sang their song again as they walked back to their sheep:

> *Life is a mystery.*
> *It's very hard to see*
> *What is real and what is true,*
> *What is me and what is you.*

So here's a question for you:
What do you think the story means?

30. The Piper's Boots

Here's a great gritty and somewhat gory story from Scotland with a brilliant twist at the end. Conjure up the main character of the travelling piper, his poverty and hunger and how he feels about being treated like dirt. Then enjoy his revenge. If you can play an instrument you can put that into the story, too. There are lots of talking points about poverty and generosity.

O nce there was a piper who travelled from town to town playing his pipes in the street for anyone who would listen. People would give him a coin or two or some food, and in that way he kept body and soul together. In summer he was fine, playing to the people working in the fields and sleeping out at night in the woods and on the haystacks. But winter was tough for the piper, especially when there was snow. In winter he worked as a carpenter doing odd jobs around people's houses in return for food and a warm bed for the night.

It was on one such winter evening that the piper was trudging along a snow-covered path. His boots were old and full of holes and his feet were wet and frozen. His belly was empty – he hadn't eaten for two days. 'Oh! What I'd give for a new pair of boots and a plate of porridge!' he thought to himself.

Just then he tripped on something under the snow and fell flat on his face. Curious as to what had tripped him, he felt under the snow and found a boot, but when he tried to pull it out of the snow it wouldn't move. Scooping away the snow he found a leg connected to the boot, and a body connected to the leg, then a head and arms connected to the body. It was a dead body frozen solid in the snow!

The piper looked at the glistening face and frowned. 'That'll be me soon,' he thought, 'if I don't get some food inside me.'

Then the piper noticed the man's boots – they were almost new and made of fine soft leather. 'These will suit me just fine!' he said. 'He won't need them now!' He tried to pull one of the boots off. He pulled and pulled but it was stuck fast, frozen solid. 'Just one thing for it then!' he thought, took out his saw and sawed through the legs of the corpse just above the boots. He put the boots with the feet in them into his bag and walked off down the road imagining how good his feet would feel in the new boots once they has defrosted.

A mile down the road the piper came to a farmhouse. He looked through the window and saw a table piled high with food: meat, fish, potatoes and gravy. His mouth watered at the sight of so much food even before he could smell the delicious aromas from under the door.

He knocked on the door and a farmer answered with a scowl on his face. 'Beggars are not welcome here!' he snapped and slammed the door shut in the piper's face.

'I'm not a beggar, I'm a piper!' he shouted at the closed door and knocked again.

When the door swung open again he said, 'Please sir, it's a freezing night. I have nowhere to sleep and nothing to eat. Please spare me a crust and a place out of the cold.'

The farmer was about to slam the door a second time when the farmer's wife came over to the door. 'Let the piper sleep in the barn!' she said. 'It's freezing out. Off you go to the barn and be off with you first thing in the morning. It's safe in the barn but keep away from the black cow. She sometimes bites strangers!'

The door shut a second time and the piper went off to the barn. Keeping his distance from the black cow who was fast asleep by the door, he settled down on a bed of straw. Just then he remembered the frozen boots and feet and went over to the cow and slipped them under the sleeping cow so they would thaw out by morning.

Before dawn he woke up, pulled out the boots from under the cow, and slipped them easily off the feet and onto his own feet. They fitted just right.

But what to do with the sawn-off feet? Just then he remembered how the farmer's wife had said that the black cow was a biter, and he decided to play a little trick on them.

He slipped the sawn-off feet into his old boots and put them next to the cow's head with the bloody cut stumps pointing towards its mouth and then hid up in the hayloft above the cow and waited.

Soon after this the cock crowed and the farmer's wife came into the barn with a bucket to milk the cow. When she saw the boots in front of the cow she shrieked, 'Husband! Husband! Come quickly! Come and see!'

The farmer rushed over to the barn. 'What is it, wife?'

'Look!' she said. 'The cow has eaten the piper! There's only his boots left!'

'Oh dear,' he said. 'There'll be trouble if the police hear about that. What'll we do?' 'Let's bury the boots next to the barn. Then nobody will ever know!'

They went out behind the barn, dug a hole, threw in the boots and feet, filled in the earth again and piled the snow back on top, then went back to the farmhouse for a glass of whisky.

As they were drinking they heard the sound of bagpipes being played. Looking out the window they saw the piper standing exactly at the place where they had buried the boots, staring at them with cold angry eyes.

'GHOST!' he shouted. 'GHOST!' she shouted.

They shot out of the door and down the lane as fast as their legs could carry them, with the piper walking behind still playing. When they were out of sight he walked back to the farmhouse, sat down at the kitchen table and helped himself to a full and hearty breakfast.

The piper had just finished his breakfast when there was a knock at the door. He opened it and saw an old man, cold and shivering.

'Come in!' said the piper, and warm your feet at the fire.

The old man shook his head. 'I'll come in, but I can't warm my feet. Someone has cut them off!'

31. Midas's Wish

This is the first of two Midas stories from Ancient Greece, where the king gets the Midas touch. It's a powerful story. Conjure up the greedy and foolish king, and then how wonder and joy turns to horror as he realises what his wish means. You might explain about Dionysus first and what the God of Wine might be like. Talking points: booze and gold.

Once... there was a king who loved gold. One day he was walking through his forest when he saw a creature with a goat's body and a human head sleeping under a bush. 'I know this creature,' said the king, 'This is a friend of Dionysus, God of Wine. Let us take him to the god's temple.'

So the servants picked up the creature and carried him to the temple of Dionysus, deep in the forest. When they arrived the god appeared, with his little horns poking through his curly hair.

King Midas bowed. 'Great God, we found your friend sleeping in the forest and returned him to you.'

'Why thank you!' said Dionysus. 'That is good. Last night he drank so much wine he just fell asleep. We lost him in the forest. Thank you. Now, what would you like as a reward?'

Midas thought for a moment. 'I just love gold. What I'd really like is to have more gold than anyone in the world. I'd like it that whatever I touch turns to gold. Can you arrange that for me?'

Dionysus grinned. 'Do you really want that?' 'Oh yes please!'

'Then it shall be done.'

The god disappeared with his goat-friend, and Midas set off for the palace. 'I wonder if this will work?' he said to himself. He reached down and touched a flower. To his delight it turned to gold – gold petals, gold stem and gold leaves. He was so happy he started to sing:

> *Gold! Gold! I love gold!*
> *It makes me feel so fine.*
> *Whatever I touch it'll turn to gold*
> *And it will all be MINE!*

He walked a bit further, singing his song, then reached out and touched a tree.

A wave of gold rippled out from his finger, along the branches, down the twigs and into every leaf. It was a solid gold tree!

'Wow!' he thought. 'I'm the richest in the world.' He skipped back to the palace singing his song.

Back home he opened the gate. It turned to gold! He opened the door – it turned to gold!

'I'm hungry,' he said. 'Bring me food!' He sat at a table and waited. They brought him a plate of meat. He picked up a piece and popped it in his mouth, but his teeth broke against the solid metal. 'OWW!' he shouted.

He picked up a cup to drink away the taste. It turned to gold. He poured the wine in his mouth and it turned to thick wet gold. He spat it out on the table – gold mixed with blood.

Then his daughter rushed in. 'What is it, Dad? What's the matter?' 'Get away from me!' he roared.

But it was too late! She reached out to hug him and froze, turned from flesh and blood to a solid metal statue.

'OH NO!' he groaned. 'I love her more than gold! More than anything! Please Dionysus, take my wish back! Can it all be reversed? Please take back my power, and turn all those things back the way they were!'

Dionysus heard and smiled. 'As you wish,' he said.

The daughter and the meat and the wine and the door, the gate and the tree and the flower all returned to normal.

The king smiled at his daughter as she hugged him. 'Why are you crying, Dad?' she asked, puzzled.

'I'm just happy to see you,' he said.

32. Midas and Apollo

Here's the second half of the Midas story, where foolish Midas shares his bad taste with a god and bears the consequences. Lots of follow-up options on music, taste, points of view and dealing with shame. It works well as a comedy. I love Ted Hughes's treatment in his retelling of Ovid's Metamorphoses.

After his trouble with gold, Midas spent a lot of time in the forest. He made friends with Pan and loved to dance to his pipes. Midas would dance and dance with Pan's half-men, half-goat friends. He was happy there.

Pan was very proud of his music. 'I play the best music in the world!' he boasted one day. 'Better even that Apollo himself.'

Apollo appeared immediately with his cosmic lyre. 'Really!' he said. 'Do you think that?' 'Oh yes,' said Pan, 'definitely!'

'Fine!' snapped Apollo. 'Then we will have a competition! Let the mountain be the judge!'

Midas and the goat men sat and watched. First Pan played his jigs and dance songs. They loved it and jumped up and danced to the tunes. At the end they clapped. 'Very good!' shouted Midas. Apollo looked at him darkly.

'Next!' said the mountain. Apollo picked up his lyre and began to play. He played everything. He played joy and sorrow, light and dark, creation and destruction, love and hate, war and peace, beauty and ugliness. He played it all – everything in the universe. It was so powerful nobody could breathe. It was the most incredible thing ever played before or since. At the end the goat men sat in silence.

'Apollo wins!' said the mountain.

'Oh no!' said Midas, 'I liked Pan's music better. Apollo was so boring...'

'Really?' said Apollo. 'You listen like a donkey, so now you will look like a donkey too.'

Two donkey's ears sprouted where Midas's human ears had been. All the goat men laughed. Midas borrowed a big hat and put it over his ears so no one could see.

From that day he wore the hat all the time. Nobody in the palace knew why, except the barber. Once a month he came to cut the king's hair and saw the donkey's ears sprouting from his head. 'Tell anyone,' said the king, 'and you'll be sorry!'

The barber so wanted to tell someone the secret. Everyone in the city was talking about the king and why he always wore a hat. Was he going bald? Was he getting sick? Was it the new fashion? The barber heard all this and was BURSTING with his story but was too frightened to tell, so one day he went deep into the forest, dug a hole, and sang into the hole:

> *Donkey's ears! Donkey's ears! The king's got donkey's ears!*
> *They're big and hairy. It's just as clear as that!*
> *The king's got donkey's ears. That's why he wears a hat!*

He sang it for a while till he felt better then filled in the hole and went home. Soon reeds grew where he had dug the hole. Sometimes the reeds seemed to be singing:

> *Donkey's ears! Donkey's ears! The king's got donkey's ears!...*

One day some musicians were travelling through the wood and they cut some reeds to make new flutes. The next day they played in Midas's palace. But when the musicians started to play, they found that all the reed flutes were singing a song of their own. As they blew the flutes they seemed to sing a song:

Donkey's ears! Donkey's ears! The king's got donkey's ears!...

Everybody listened in silence, staring at the king and his hat. Midas stood frozen to the spot, his heart beating like a drum. What should he do? Then he smiled. 'It's true!' he said. 'Look!' Midas whipped off his hat and everyone gaped at the donkey's ears. There were a few sniggers but then everyone clapped.

'Bravo!' they called.
'Such courage!' said another.
'Long live the king!' said the third.

Midas took a bow, smiled and then started to sing along with the flutes:

Donkey's ears, donkey's ears, I've got donkey's ears!
They're big and hairy. It's just as clear as that!
I've got donkey's ears. That's why I wear a hat!

And that's the end of that!

33. Theseus and the Minotaur

This killing-the-monster story remains a favourite, combining heroism and horror and a love interest in a powerful mix. Here's a more extended text for you to take ideas from for your telling.

A very long time ago a war broke out between Crete and Greece. The war lasted for ten years – ten years of killing, ten years of looting, of burning and all manner of terror. After ten years Minos, the king of Crete, went down to the sea and he prayed to his father, Zeus. Minos called up to the sky, 'Father, help me! End this war and punish the Greeks for what they have done!' The sky rumbled and flashed, and Minos knew he'd been heard.

In Greece the ground began to shake and as it shook the houses began to topple one on top of another and people inside were squashed by the falling rubble. The place where the water came from – the springs – closed up and there was no more water to drink. The people of Athens were desperate, their city was being destroyed, and they knew that they should go to Minos to seek peace.

When they asked Minos if he had a price for peace, he said, 'You have hurt me. You have hurt my sons and daughters. You have hurt my people. My price is that you will remember that pain, and this is the way – once every nine years, send me a boat with fifteen young men and women on it. I will take those young people and place them in the Labyrinth under my palace. They may enter but they will never leave, for down there, there is the Minotaur, half- bull, half-man. He will devour them! Send them once every nine years and you will have peace. Refuse and it will be war – this time with my father Zeus fighting with me!'

The Greeks agreed, feeling they had no choice, and so it began. Once every nine years a black-sailed ship set off from Athens and sailed through the islands to Crete. Fifteen young men and women were wined and dined by Minos, and then locked inside the Labyrinth never to leave. It was a great weight and a great sorrow for the people of Greece, and one for which they saw no end.

Then a hero came to Greece. His name was Theseus, adopted son to the king. He was a man who liked to fight and who liked to win, and he liked to brag about his victory. The Greeks saw him as a hero, a great hero, and he was worshiped as if he was a king. His strength was famous.

They say the first time Theseus came into Athens, with his long hair down to his shoulders, two workmen on the roof of a house looked down thinking him a woman and said, 'Oh! There's a pretty young girl!' It happened that a cow was walking past him in the street, and they say that Theseus took hold of the cow with one hand and threw it higher than the building where the men were working. After that the men kept quiet. The story spread around the city and around the country, and everyone was pleased that Greece had such a hero.

Well, the year came round, the ninth year, when the black-sailed ship was to sail for Crete. Theseus went to the king and said, 'Father, let me go as one of the fifteen. I will kill this creature and finish with this problem once and for all.'

'No,' said the king, 'it is too dangerous. Anyone who goes there never returns.'

'Father,' said Theseus, 'I have not been defeated by any of the tasks that you have set me, what makes you think that I will fail now?'

So Theseus joined the young men and women and together they sailed down to the island of Crete. Minos welcomed them on the shore and said, 'Welcome, my friends! It is our last night together before you go to the Labyrinth. Let us eat and dance.' And Minos laid on a great banquet. All of his relatives were there, his wife, his sons and his daughters, and they all listened in amazement to Theseus as he bragged about his adventures and his battles and the things that he had done. They were surprised because he wasn't frightened – he was full of confidence. But one of Minos's daughters, Ariadne, looked at him in a different way. She looked at his long hair, his eyes, his nose, his chin. She found it all quite lovely.

When everyone had gone to sleep, she sneaked into Theseus's room, sat on the edge of his bed and gave his leg a little shake.
'Oh, what is it?' he said.
'Theseus!' she said. 'Theseus! Do you think I'm pretty?' 'Yeah, you're quite pretty,' he said.
'Theseus, if you like me, I like you too. Maybe I can help you?' 'Well, what kind of help do you want to give me?'
'Well, I know how to get into the Labyrinth and how to get out, and if you take me with you when you go I'll tell you.'
'Alright then, I promise.'
'This is it, you see – I've got a ball of silver thread and I tie it to the door when I go in, and I just unwind the thread as I go deeper and deeper into the Labyrinth and then, when I want to leave, I just follow the thread back. It's easy really, I'll show you. We can go now if you like.'
'Alright then,' he said. 'Let's go now! Let's do it now!'

Theseus took the ball of thread and went to the entrance of the Labyrinth. He tied the thread around the door lintel and walked down into the passage. Deeper and deeper into the earth, darker and danker, until he could hear nothing but the beating of his own heart and the drip, drip of water from the ceiling to the stone floor.

What happened in the Labyrinth no one knows exactly but later Theseus emerged from the Labyrinth winding back that thread, with blood on his sword and a smile on his face. Ariadne was there. She said, 'Theseus, is it done? Can we go now?'

'Yes,' he said, 'it's done. Let's leave.'

So Theseus took Ariadne and the other young people who'd come with him. They went to the harbour and they took that black-sailed boat and started sailing back towards Athens.

Ariadne was so happy, this was her first boyfriend, and she really liked him. She really loved him! That first night she snuggled up next to Theseus in the boat looking at the stars thinking how romantic it all was, how lovely everything was, how she was going to live happily ever after with Theseus. But Theseus had other ideas. As Ariadne lay next to him in the boat he fell asleep and in his dream he dreamt of the God of Wine – the God Dionysus. In the dream, Dionysus spoke. 'Theseus, this girl, Ariadne, she's very lovely but you don't need her now. You've got what you want and she's what I want, so do me a favour. Tomorrow as you go past the island of Naxos, drop her off there. I'm having a party there and I'd really like her to come. Do it for me, Theseus, and I won't forget you. Do it for me.'

In the morning Theseus woke and said to his men, 'Sail for Naxos! We'll rest there.' When the boat landed he said to Ariadne, 'My dear, why don't you pick some shells on the beach for a while? We've got things to do and then we'll leave.'

Ariadne said, 'OK, darling, I'll go and collect those shells with the holes in the middle and I'll make you a necklace because I love you so much.'

'Yeah,' he said. 'Great. You do that.'

But when Ariadne had got to the edge of the beach Theseus and his men and the young people got back into the boat and it sailed away. Ariadne couldn't believe her eyes! She called out, 'Theseus, wait! Wait for me!' But he didn't even turn his head. She understood she'd been betrayed. She grew angry and clenched her fist at him, and then called to the sky, 'Grandfather Zeus! Grandfather Zeus! This man! Look what he's done to me! He's taken me from my family! He's promised me and then he's betrayed me! Let his ambition turn bitter in his mouth! Do that for me, Grandfather Zeus, let his pride turn bitter!' And the sky rumbled and she knew that she had been heard and she watched as the black- sailed ship disappeared over the horizon.

As the black-sailed ship carried Theseus back to Greece, he was imagining his welcome. Imagining the crowds in the streets calling his name, shouting his praises. He was thinking how the stories would be passed from place to place, from storyteller to storyteller, until he would be the greatest hero of all Greece. He was so busy with these thoughts that he forgot to change the colour of the sails. Now, the king was waiting for his son up on the cliffs above the port, and when he saw the black-sailed ship returning he thought his stepson dead. Such was his grief that he fell from the cliff, twisting and turning through the air and then breaking his back on the rocks below.

In this way Theseus was welcomed home, not with a banquet, but with a funeral. The city was in mourning for their king and he joined the mourners. In this way the taste of victory turned bitter in his own mouth. Zeus had taken revenge for his betrayal of Ariadne.

34. Icarus

Icarus is a useful story for so many reasons. On the one hand it is about foolish risk-taking and on the other about listening to others and taking advice when needed. This boundary between safety and thrills, obedience and autonomy, is important for us all. This simple tale is great to explore for these reasons, not to mention the science topics of flight and wings. There are lots of great role play options between parent and child. You might explain, before starting, a little about the Minotaur story as background and the Ancient Greeks in general.

When Theseus killed the Minotaur, King Minos was furious. Theseus had killed his son and stolen his daughter away from right under his nose! Someone was to blame! Someone had to pay! And that someone was Daedalus the Smith, the man who had made the labyrinth. Minos summoned Daedalus.

'How can I help your majesty?' Daedalus smiled, confident as usual.

'All this is your fault!' snapped the king. 'You were told to build a maze so tangled that all who entered would never leave. Weren't you?'

'Yes, your majesty,' he argued, still calm. 'But you saw the thread, no maze can defeat a thread, however perfect.'

'I don't want excuses, and anyway I hear you were mixed up somehow with the queen in making that bull-headed child in the first place! What do you have to say about THAT?' Daedalus hung his head. 'Nothing, your majesty. I only do what I am told to do. I cannot be responsible for what my superiors do with my creations...'

Minos shook his head. 'No, blacksmith! You make them, you are responsible, and this time you will pay! You and your son can spend some time in my prison while I think about what to do with you. Guards!'

Daedalus and Icarus were taken to the prison tower which the blacksmith himself had designed and built, and were locked inside the highest cell with a lock that Daedalus himself had made.

His son didn't like it there. 'Dad,' he whined, 'I want to go home.'

Daedalus patted the boy on his shoulder. 'Don't worry son, give me a week and I'll solve the problem.'

Every day Daedalus took half of the bread the guards gave them to eat, and scattered it on the window sill of the cell.

Icarus was curious. 'Dad, what are you doing? I'm hungry.' 'Wait and see,' came the reply.

When the birds came to feed on the bread, Daedalus would crouch like a cat by the window and every now and then pounce on a bird, pull out its longest feathers, let it go and wait for the next bird. After a week he had a great pile of feathers.

In the evenings he saved half of the wax from the candles the guards gave them, and when he had saved enough, he started working, sticking the feathers together with the wax, making two huge pairs of wings.

As ever, he was proud of his creation. 'Look son, these wings will take us away from here, to a new land with a new king to serve. But you have to be careful.'

'Don't worry, Dad!'

'No! Listen, Icarus! This is important! The wings are made from wax and feathers. They are weak! You have to be careful! Fly straight and steady next to me and you'll be fine, but don't do anything else. Fly too high and the wax will melt in the sun's heat. Fly too low and the sea will wet the feathers and you will fall. Stay with me and we'll both be fine.'

'Don't worry, Dad, I'll be alright.'

With the wings strapped to their arms and shoulders they stood, perched for a moment on the window ledge. Below them a bull bellowed, above them an eagle hovered.

'Now!'

Together they fell into space, their wings catching the updraft of their falling. Their falling slowed and then, meeting a pocket of rising air, they climbed with it, above the tower and glided, wingtip to wingtip, north over the cliffs, out over the ocean.

Icarus was delighted and excited. 'Look, Dad! Look what I can see! Look down there, dolphins! This is great!'

'Just stay straight and steady.'

For some time they flew together, till Icarus grew restless. 'Dad, look what I can do!'

Icarus turned a somersault in mid-air.

'No, son! It's dangerous. The wings aren't strong enough. Stay by me!' 'Dad, you worry too much! Look! Watch me climb!'

Icarus began to spiral up above his father, ignoring the pleas to return. He climbed higher and higher into the heat of the sun until he felt the drip of liquid wax on his shoulder and, in an instant, the feathers were gone. He plummeted like a falling anvil, down past his father, smashing into the sea with such force that his spine snapped.

Daedalus hovered and watched his son's lifeless body floating in the water below, adding his own tears to the sea's stock of salt, as he felt, for the first time, the suffering which his own creations had caused.

35. The Woman of the Sea

This is another selkie story from Scotland, where seals turn to women and back again. A swell as the magic of the transformation, there are the resonances of separation and reunion in the family: lots of strong feelings to evoke with the divided family.

One summer evening a young man was walking along a long, wide sandy beach, under a full moon, next to a quiet shining sea. He had been working all day in the fields cutting and binding the hay. Hot and sweaty, he thought to go for a swim. In front of him in the moonlight he heard the sound of strange music and saw a group of women dancing on the beach. He stopped and hid behind a rock as they danced to strange flowing music. It seemed to come from instruments made of shells and seaweed. The women rose and fell together like crashing waves. He had never seen anything so beautiful. Beside the dancers he saw a pile of sealskins, glistening in the moonlight.

'These must be seal-women,' he thought. 'I have heard about them. Sometimes they are seals and sometimes they are human.'

He crept closer and saw that they had no shadows in the bright moonlight. When his own shadow touched the circle they turned as one and stared, like a shoal of startled fish, then rushed for their sealskins, ran into the waves and, slipping on the skins, became seals once more. But one of the seal-women could not find her skin and ran up and down the beach looking for it. The man realised it was next to his feet and, quickly, he picked it up and hid it behind a rock.

'Come here!' he said. 'Let me help you!'

She ran to him, out of breath. 'I've lost my skin! Help me find it!'

'Alright,' he said, and walked up and down the beach with her till morning. 'It's gone!' he said. 'Come home with me instead. Be my wife!'

'But I cannot come. My family is there in the sea! I cannot leave my children!'

'Maybe one day you will find your skin,' he said, 'but till then, come and live with me. Be my human wife.'

She was frightened and nodded, waving out to the cluster of seals bobbing around in the waves as she walked away.

For seven years she cared for his house – cleaning and cooking and looking after the three young children she gave birth to. The man was happy to have such a beautiful wife. Every evening after work it was a delight to come home. Even if she was always a little sad, she never complained and, after a while, he stopped noticing.

Every evening she'd go down to the sea and stare out over the waves. Sometimes a seal head would appear and call out to her from the waves.

Then she would sing to them:

> *Take me home, Mother Sea! Take me home!*
> *Take me home, Mother Sea! Take me home!*
> *Let me be in the waves of your sweet flowing heart.*
> *Take me home, Mother Sea! Take me home!*

In the day, when he was at work, she'd cook and clean, singing that same song to herself as she worked. And in the evening she sang her children to sleep with it in their beds:

> *Take me home, Mother Sea! Take me home!...*

Then, one winter day, she was playing hide and seek with her children on the beach when one of them found a dark skin under a rock.

'Mum, what's this? It's so soft and dark!'

She looked at her home. She looked at her children. She looked at the sea. She hugged each child and ran to the water, slipping on her skin. The next moment there was just a seal head bobbing in the waves. The children ran to the waves and called, 'Mother, come back! Don't leave us!' They watched as a group of seals swam to her and then they all disappeared under the waves.

From that day on the home was sad. The children helped to cook and clean and every evening they'd go down to the sea and sing:

Take me home, Mother Sea! Take me home!...

One day she came for them, with three small skins, and they were gone, leaving the husband alone with only his memories for the rest of his days. On clear nights he'd go to the beach and wait and hope, but the seal-woman never returned.

36. How Jerusalem Began

I love this version of how Jerusalem began. It is claimed variously by Palestinian, Jewish and Christian communities around the world. You can read another version penned by myself in One City, Two Brothers *from Barefoot Books. It's a fable of love, generosity and sacred place. It is quite a tricky tale to tell. Pay attention to the detail of what happens when and make the physical description really clear. Build up suspense in the first half – what is going on?*

Once, on opposite sides of a hill, were two villages. Between the villages was a field where two brothers farmed together. The elder lived in one with his wife and children. The younger lived in the other village. He was single and lived alone.

Every spring the brothers ploughed the land and sowed it with wheat, then watered and weeded till the grain was golden. Then they cut and threshed the crop, pouring the grain into bags and tying up the straw into sheaves of hay for the animals. Every year they divided it all half and half.

One summer they had just divided the harvest, fifteen sacks of grain each, and had carted off the sacks to their own villages. The elder brother thought, 'My little brother needs this grain more than me. When he's old he won't have any children to look after him. I know what I'll do. I'll sneak these extra bags into his grain store tonight and he'll get a surprise in the morning.'

That night the elder brother loaded three sacks onto the top of his donkey, climbed up over the top of the hill and down to his brother's village, and sneaked the bags into his brother's store.

The next morning the elder brother said to his wife, 'We have just twelve sacks to last us for the year. That's one sack every month. That will be plenty!'

'Hmmm...' she said, 'I thought there was more than that?' She went into her husband's store and came back a while later, puzzled. 'Husband, there are fifteen sacks in there, not twelve. You must be tired after all that work!'

He went and counted and sure enough there were fifteen. 'How strange!' he thought. 'I must have dreamt it. I'll give him the bags tonight.'

So that night he loaded up his donkey and walked to his little brother's house, slipped the three sacks in the store and came home.

The next morning he told his wife what he had done, but when she looked into the store she saw there were still fifteen sacks. 'What are you up to?' she asked, 'Is this a trick?' The elder brother was confused now, but was determined to give away the sacks. That evening he set off down the hill for the third time, towards his brother's home.

Two nights earlier the younger brother was just unloading his sacks of grain when he thought, 'My elder brother needs this more than me. He has a family to feed and I'm by myself. I know what I'll do. I'll give him a surprise!' That night he loaded three sacks of grain onto his donkey and led it quietly up and over the hill to his brother's home, slipped the sacks into the store and came home, smiling.

The next day he noticed that there were still fifteen sacks in his store. 'Strange!' he thought. 'I'll give them to him tonight anyway.'

So the next night he led his donkey up and over the hill to his brother's village and put three more sacks into his store. But the next day there was still fifteen sacks in his own grain store.

'What's going on?' he thought. 'Is this some magic trick, or am I just imagining that I give the sacks away every night? Anyway, third time lucky!'

He loaded up his donkey that night with three more sacks and set off up the hillside. As he climbed he saw someone coming towards him, looking just like his own reflection – a man with a donkey and three sacks on top. As the brothers came closer they recognised each other and understood the puzzle of the sacks, and they were filled with joy at the love they had given and received.

That holy spot where the two brothers met is the holy place where the city of Jerusalem began.

37. Odysseus and the Cyclops

Here's another popular monster tale from the Ancient Greeks. It's gritty and gory and great for action drama. Tellers can build on all their knowledge of monsters and heroes from digital sources. It's a delightful mixture of comedy and horror and of course a link into The Odyssey.

Once there was a war between the city of Troy and the armies of Greece. For ten long years the Greeks laid siege to Troy, which was finally defeated by the Greeks thanks to the cleverness of one of their kings, Odysseus.

When the war was over, Odysseus set off for home sailing from island to island on the way back to Ithaca where his wife waited for him. On one such island, Odysseus had anchored his boat offshore and rowed to the beach with a party of twelve men in order to look around for food. After a while they came to a cave packed full with sheep and goats. Odysseus and his men waited in the cave for the owner of the sheep to arrive so they could offer to buy a few for their journey.

Around nightfall a huge one-eyed giant, Polyphemus, returned to the cave to check on his sheep and immediately smelled the presence of humans inside. 'Who's in there?' he roared. 'Come out and show yourself or, when I catch you, I will stick you on a spit and roast you for supper!'

Nobody came out, and the cave was too small for the giant to get in, but he reached into the cave, grabbed two of the men and ate them, there and then, as the others listened to their screams. Then Polyphemus blocked the entrance to the cave with a huge stone, impossible for the men to move, and went away to sleep.

The next morning he returned, rolled away the stone, reached inside, grabbed two more of the men and devoured them. Then one by one he let the sheep and goats out of the cave, looking closely at each, one by one, to check there were no men trying to escape.

All day Odysseus thought about the situation and came up with a plan. He took a long wooden club of the giant's and sharpened one end to a fine point. Then, when the giant came back for his evening meal, Odysseus offered him some wine. 'It's good,' he said.
'The best wine in Troy. Try it!'
'I will,' said the giant. 'But tell me, what is your name?' 'Nobody,' said Odysseus. 'My name is Nobody.'
'That's a strange name,' said the giant, and started drinking.

Polyphemus drank and soon became sleepy and fell asleep in the entrance to the cave, blocking it. Odysseus and his men carried the club up to his snoring head and plunged it hard into the giant's single eye. Polyphemus screamed and bellowed and tried to find the men who had done it but they scurried back to the corner of the cave out of reach, where the giant could not get them!

So Polyphemus rolled the stone back over the cave entrance and then ran around the island in a blind drunken rage calling out, 'Nobody has blinded me! Nobody has blinded me!' and all the other giants laughed, thinking he was just being foolish. So no one came to help him.

The next morning the giant came back to the cave, rolled away the stone and started to lead the sheep out one by one. Odysseus and his men had tied themselves to the bellies of the sheep in the cave with their belts. As the sheep were led out the giant felt the coat of each, one by one, to make sure there were no men hiding, but didn't notice the men hanging underneath the sheep.

The men rushed down to their boat and rowed out to the ship. As Odysseus sailed away he shouted out to Polyphemus, 'You think I am Nobody – but I am somebody. I am Odysseus, the great warrior, remember me!'

Polyphemus did remember him. He told the story to his father, God of the Sea, Poseidon, who from that day became Odysseus's enemy, creating storms and trouble for Odysseus on his long journey home.

And that's how Odysseus escaped from the cave of the one-eyed giant, Polyphemus.

38. The Four Dragons

*Here's a Chinese story about how its four main rivers began: the Heilongjiang,
the Huang He in central China, the Yangtze, and the Zhujiang. You might
show your class a map of China with these four rivers on it as an introduction.
Dragons create huge enthusiasms. I like this one because the dragons are helpful
and compassionate, as is often the case in that part of the world. It's also a way
into discussions about the environment and the importance of water for life.*

Once, long ago, there were no rivers or lakes on the earth. The rain came and watered the land, but then disappeared underground.

In those days there were four great dragons who lived in the eastern sky – the Long Dragon, the Yellow Dragon, the Black Dragon and the Pearl Dragon. They were great friends and would spend their days flying and playing together above the earth. One day they were playing in the sky as usual when they noticed people down on earth praying.

'Please send us rain! Let the gods send us rain! If not our crops will die and then we will die of hunger. Please send rain to us so our children will have rice to eat!'

The dragons looked down and saw that the earth was as dry as a bone. Nothing could grow in such soil and all the fields were bare and dry. The people were thin and dying. The dragons could see the ribs of the children and their swollen hungry bellies.

'How poor the people are!' said the Yellow Dragon. 'They will die if it doesn't rain soon.' The Long Dragon nodded, 'Let's go and beg the Emperor for rain.'

The Emperor was chief of the gods. If anyone could help, he could. The dragons flew off to the Heavenly Palace to see the Emperor but he was not pleased to see them.

'What are you doing here without an invitation?' he said. 'Go back to the eastern sky and leave me in peace!'

The Long Dragon stepped forward and said, 'Please, your majesty, we have seen the sufferings of people on earth. Without rain they will all die. Have pity and send them rain. We come to ask for that.'

'You go away,' the Emperor said, 'and I'll send some rain down soon.'

The four dragons went happily back. But ten days passed, and not a drop of rain came down. The people suffered more, some eating bark, some grass roots, some forced to eat white clay when they ran out of bark and grass roots. Seeing all this, the four dragons felt very sorry, and realised that the Emperor only cared about pleasure, and never thought about the troubles of the people.

'So what shall we do?' said the Long Dragon.
'We have to do something ourselves. He will never help,' said the Yellow Dragon.
'How can we make it rain?' said the Pearl Dragon.
'Is there not plenty of water in the sea where we live? We should scoop it up and spray it towards the sky. The water will be like raindrops and come down to save the people and their crops,' suggested the Black Dragon.
'Good idea!' said the others as they clapped their hands.
'But,' said the Long Dragon after thinking a bit, 'we will be blamed if the Emperor learns of this.'
'I will do anything to save the people,' the Yellow Dragon said.
'Then let's begin. We will never regret it,' said Long Dragon.

The dragons flew to the sea, scooped up water in their mouths and on their wings, and then flew back into the sky, where they sprayed the water out over the earth. The four dragons flew back and forth, making the sky dark all around. Before long the sea water became rain pouring down from the sky.

'It's raining! It's raining! The crops will be saved!' the people cried and leaped with joy.

On the ground the wheat stalks raised their heads and the rice stalks straightened up. The people were happy, but then the Sea God reported what had happened to the Emperor.

'How dare the four dragons bring rain without my permission!' he fumed.

The Emperor ordered his armies to arrest the four dragons. Being far outnumbered, the four dragons could not defend themselves, and they were soon arrested and brought back to the Heavenly Palace.

'Go and get four mountains to lay upon them so that they can never escape!' the Emperor ordered the Mountain God.

The Mountain God used his magic power to make four mountains fly there, and pressed them down on top of the four dragons. Imprisoned as they were, they did not for one moment regret what they had done. Instead they worked some dragon magic, and turned themselves into four rivers, which flowed from the four high mountains down the mountain valleys, crossing the whole land from the west to the east and finally emptying into the sea.

This is how China's four great rivers were formed – the Heilongjiang (Black Dragon) in the far north, the Huang He (Yellow River) in central China, the Changjiang (Yangtze, or Long River) farther south, and the Zhujiang (Pearl) in the south.

So when the rain stops for a while, people can take water from the rivers to make their crops grow. All thanks to those four dragons.

39. The Land of the Deep Ocean

Here's another careful-what-you-wish-for story, this time from Japan, which plays with the idea of time being different in different places. Our kind hero travels to a wonderful undersea world and lives happily for a while, until restlessness is his undoing. Try and conjure the wonder and wonderfulness of the other world, and then the growing horror as he returns home to his doom! Hear Rafe Martin tell this one on his Yellow Moon CD.

Once, on the edge of the great ocean, there was a beach. Next to the beach was a village and in the village was a wooden house. Inside the house there lived a fisherman. He was single, but happy enough and loved spending the evenings with his brothers and sisters and parents, all of whom lived close by in the same village. Every morning he'd row his boat out into the sea, cast his nets, pull them in and sell whatever he caught at the village market. In this way time passed happily.

Then one day he was walking down the beach when he saw a group of children crowded around something, jeering and throwing stones. Coming closer he saw that they had surrounded a huge turtle, which was as long as the fisherman was tall. It was trying to get back to the sea but the children were blocking its way.

The fisherman called out, 'Why do you hurt this innocent creature?'
'Why not?' said their leader. 'There's nothing else to do here.'
'Leave him,' he said. 'Let me give you a few coins and you can go and spend them in the market.'

The children grinned, pocketed the coins and ran off down the beach, while the turtle waddled down to the sea and swam out through the waves. He turned and stared intently at the fisherman before he dived underwater and was gone.

The next morning the fisherman rowed out into the ocean, dropped his nets and waited. It was a gentle, warm day and he fell asleep in the boat, fell into a deep and lovely dream. He dreamt of a beautiful young woman with eyes as green as seaweed, skin as fair as beach sand and hair as black as a seagull's eye. In the dream she rose up out of the water, walked towards him in his boat and touched him on the shoulder. At that moment he woke up and there she was with him in the boat!

'Who are you?' he asked, astonished.

'I am the daughter of the Sea King who lives in the land of the deep ocean. He was that turtle. You helped him and now he will help you. He has sent me to be your bride. If you wish, you can come home with me to live in the Kingdom of the Deep. Would you like that? But if you come you may never return.'

He nodded. He had never seen anything so beautiful. She leaned over and kissed him softly on the lips and he felt his world explode.

Together they dived into the water and, taking his hand, she swam with him down to the deep ocean, down through a tunnel and up into a vast cave filled with all the creatures of the sea.

'Welcome, Good Man!' the sea creatures called to him. 'Welcome to our kingdom!'

The fisherman and the Sea King's daughter were married and lived happily for a while in the king's palace, playing with the fish and dolphins, swimming out into the deep ocean and exploring the tunnels and caves of the sea bed. The fisherman had never been so full of joy and life.

In this way the years passed and he began to think of his family and friends in the village. He wanted to see them. The more he thought about it the bigger this want became until he could bear it no longer.

'Let me go back home,' he said to his wife. 'Let me see my family again.'
'I told you there was no way back!' she said softly.
'Please! There must be a way. I cannot live here as a prisoner!'
She nodded sadly. 'If you must go then take this box with you – it will protect you as long as you never open it. But believe me, you'd be happier here.'
It was a tiny black box the size of a matchbox.

They swam up to the surface of the sea and the Sea King's daughter led the fisherman to the beach by his village, waving sadly goodbye as he clutched the black box in his hand. He was so excited at the thought of seeing his family and friends he rushed up the beach and into the village.

Then he stopped. It all looked very different. 'I suppose it's because I've been away,' he thought. He looked up at the mountains behind the house. They were covered with tall thick trees! He remembered the mountains as being bare. He looked at the wall around his village. It was made of stone! He remembered it as being of wood. He went to the place where his own house had stood, but there was nothing there. Just an empty field!

An old man walked by.
'Excuse me,' said the fisherman, 'but what has happened to my house? I used to live here but the house has gone. What has happened?'
The old man shook his head. 'I've lived here all my life and I've never seen a house here. You must be lost. What's your name?'
The fisherman told him, 'Taro. My name is Urashimo Taro.' The old man looked at him, puzzled. 'Is this a joke?'
'No!' said the fisherman. 'That's my name.'
'There's a story here that long ago there was a man by that name who went out to sea and never returned. His family searched for him but only found an empty boat. They say he was taken by a mermaid, but that's just stories. Anyway, that

was long ago but if you don't believe me you can go to the graveyard. His family are all buried there.'

As if in a dream the fisherman walked to the graveyard on the edge of the village and looked from grave to grave. It was true – there was the gravestone of his father covered in moss and lichen. There was his mother's stone. Also his brothers and sisters and the graves of their children and grandchildren and great-grandchildren. How was it possible? It was as if he had been away not just for three years but for three hundred years. How could it be?

He walked back to the beach and stared out at the sea. He had no home, no family here. Just the little black box in his hand. Maybe that had the clue.

The fisherman carefully slid open the box and as he did so a white light spiralled up out of the box and away over the ocean.

The next moment he felt tired, then there was pain all over his body. It was hard to breathe. He felt his skin shrivel and his hair turn white. Then his skin and flesh was gone, leaving only white bone. As the skeleton fell to the ground it crumbled into dust mixing with the sand on the beach. There was no trace of the man who had once been... Urashimo Taro.

40. Rama and Sita

*This is one of the best-known stories from India from the epic
Ramayana tales and works well as a killing-the- monster tale. Conjure
up the horror of the demon and the courage of the Monkey God.
If you've got a drum, try using it to create atmosphere.*

O nce there was a great prince, Rama, who lived with his good wife, Sita, in their father's kingdom. But when the king announced that Prince Rama should become king, one of the palace queens plotted against him.

She went to the king and said, 'Your majesty, do you remember your promise to grant me a wish once we were married? Well, I have thought of my wish.'
'What is that?' said the king.
'I wish that Rama be banished from this kingdom forever and never allowed to return. I would rather that my son becomes king and not him.'

The king was sad but he had given his word and so Rama was banished. He left the city and his wife, Sita, went with him, determined to support her husband in this time of need. They lived together happily with Rama's brother, Laksman, deep in a beautiful forest. Rama was skilled with the bow, providing food and protection for Sita and his brother.

Then one day Demon King Ravana of Sri Lanka decided to kidnap the lovely Sita. He sent a golden deer into the forest. When Sita saw it she asked her husband to catch it for her so Rama ran off leaving her alone with his brother.

When Rama shot the deer it called out, 'Help me! Help me!' in a way that sounded just like Rama. When his brother heard this he thought Rama was in trouble. He told Sita to stay inside a magic circle, which he drew on the ground, so she would be safe and then he ran off into the forest, leaving Sita alone.

Moments later an old man appeared in front of Sita asking for help. 'I am tired and hungry,' he said. 'Help me!'

Sita stepped towards him – out of the circle – and at that moment he turned into an eight-headed demon. The Demon King grabbed Sita and flew up into the air, taking her away to his island.

As the Demon King Ravana travelled with Sita, the King of the Birds saw what was happening and flew up into the air and fought with Ravana, but the demon was too strong and, wounded by the many claws of the Demon King, the King of the Birds fell down to earth, dying.

At that moment Rama and his brother, Laksman, came across the bird who told them what had happened to Sita.

Rama and Laksman set off to rescue Sita. On their journey they were joined by many warriors and a race of huge monkeys. Rama sent the chief of the monkeys, Hanuman, to Sri Lanka to look for signs of Sita and to give her his ring.

Hanuman travelled to Sri Lanka, leapt across the sea to the island and found Sita, trapped in prison. When he gave her Rama's ring she knew he was alive and coming to find her.

After that, huge Hanuman started to rampage in the city, destroying many buildings with a huge club until he was shot with an arrow, captured and sentenced to death by burning. But, as the fire was lit it burned the city, not Hanuman. He leapt away from the island and returned to Rama to tell his story.

When Rama and his armies arrived at the shore near Sri Lanka they could not get across the sea but the giant monkeys threw huge stones into the sea, building a causeway from the land to the island.

When Rama and his armies finally reached Sri Lanka the two armies faced each other in battle.

Rama was victorious, and when Demon King Ravana tried to run away he was caught and crushed by two rocks. Inside the rocks were the souls of his daughters who he had murdered. In this way they took their revenge.

Sita was freed and reunited with her husband. After fourteen years away, they returned home to their city and Rama finally ruled as king.

41. The Building of St Paul's Cathedral

This little fable can be used to explore what makes us happy and the need to make a contribution to the greater good. Simple and powerful. It can also link to history and architecture if you like.

In 1666 London was burned to the ground in the Great Fire of London. Afterwards the architect, Sir Christopher Wren, designed a new building for the heart of the city. It was to be an enormous cathedral, dedicated to St Paul, with a huge domed roof, bigger than any that had been built before. It was to be a place for prayer and meditation.

During the building of the Cathedral, Christopher Wren went to visit the site. He noticed three men working building a wall – bricklayers – lifting and setting the stone blocks in cement. Two of them were frowning and a third was smiling.

Curious, Sir Christopher went over to the men for a chat. He asked the first frowning builder, 'What are you doing?'
'I'm doing what I'm told,' the builder answered, crossly. 'Building a wall. Isn't that obvious? If I didn't I wouldn't get paid.'

He asked the second frowning builder the same question. 'I'm earning money so that I can feed my family!' he snapped.

Finally, Sir Christopher asked the man who worked with a smile on his face, 'What are you doing?'

'I am building the most beautiful building in London,' he replied with a smile. 'For hundreds of years to come people from all over the world will visit this magnificent building and admire its beauty. They will feel inspired, uplifted and find peace here. I am playing my part in making all that happen.'

If you go to London and visit St Paul's Cathedral you will see that it is still there, still a beautiful place for prayer and meditation.

Which builder would you rather be?

42. Feathers in the Wind

I heard this story first from the wonderful Doug Lipman. It's from the Jewish tradition and offers a chance to reflect on unwise speech and the spreading ripples of consequences. Evoke the gossiper in a way appropriate to your class.

Once upon a time there was a village. In that village, like most villages, there was a woman who loved to gossip. Every day she would sit with her friends gossiping about the bad things she said others had done. 'Can you believe he did that?' 'Can you believe she said that?' and 'Did you see what he was wearing? A man of his age!' On and on and on she would gossip.

The stories spread around the village and caused much trouble. Friends became enemies, husband and wife became separate, parents grew angry with their children, and all because of the gossip that came from this one lady.

One day the Rabbi asked to see her.
'Will you do something for me?' he asked. 'Of course, Rabbi. What can I do?'
'Please take this cushion, go outside, cut it open and release all the feathers, and then come back in.'
'But why?' she asked.
'Just do as I ask,' he told her.

The woman went outside, slit the cushion open and released all the feathers into the wind. She watched them billow up into the air and away into the distance. She made sure all the feathers were gone and then walked back inside to the Rabbi.

'Job done!' she said. 'Anything else I can help with?'

'Yes please. Just one more thing. I would like you to go out and bring back all the feathers.' 'What? But I can't!' she said. 'They've been blown all over the place – down the street, over the hill and far away. I'll never be able to bring them back.' 'True!' said the Rabbi. 'And so it is with words and idle gossip. Words once spoken can never be taken back. There is no telling how far they will travel and what harm they will do. From now on, I want you to think before you speak.'

And so she did.

43. Heaven and Hell [1]

This is a well-known Japanese story often found in many Zen collections. I love its simplicity and hopefulness. For the story to work you have to evoke the outrage and anger of the warrior so the audience is drawn into his fury, then the shift to silence and respect as he understands the lesson. May we all learn it!

A samurai warrior, famous for his courage and skill, went to see a wise monk. 'Teach me about heaven and hell!' commanded the warrior..

The holy man frowned.
'Certainly not, you are a violent and stupid man. You would not understand!'

The warrior flushed with anger.
'How dare you talk to me like that!' he said.

'You think you are so important!' retorted the monk. 'But you are nothing but a pathetic worm! Go away and leave me alone.'

'Nobody talks to me like that and gets away with it,' said the warrior. 'One more word out of you and this sword will slice through your neck!'

'You dog,' laughed the holy man. 'You wouldn't dare!'

Furious, the warrior drew back his sword and was about to strike, when the wise monk raised a finger and smiled:

'That, my friend, is hell.'

The warrior dropped his sword and bowed.

'Thank you,' he said. 'You are indeed wise, and have shown me my weakness. Thank you!'

'And that,' said the monk, 'is heaven.'

44. Heaven and Hell [2]

This one is often told within the Christian tradition. Again, it is a simple and enduring image, so work on clarity of description when you tell it.

Once there was a man who, having lived a good life, died and was met at the gates of heaven by St Peter.

'Where would you like to live?' asked St Peter. 'Heaven or hell?' 'I don't know,' said the man. 'What's the difference?'

'Let me show you,' said St Peter.

They flew down for a while until they came to hell. 'Look!' said St Peter. 'It's nearly time to eat.'

People were sitting at long wooden tables piled high with wonderful food. But there was something strange about it. Each person had two long wooden spoons strapped to their arms, so that their arms where effectively twice as long.

When the food bell ran they started trying to eat with the spoons, but however hard they tried they could not get a single mouthful of food into their mouth. All the food ended up on the floor as the people wailed with frustration and hunger.

'Those are the spoons of hell,' said St Peter. 'Now let's go to heaven.' They flew up to heaven and went inside.

'This is heaven,' said St Peter.

The man was puzzled. It looked exactly the same as the last room.

People were sitting at long tables piled high with wonderful food. Each person had long spoons strapped to their arms just as before.

Then the food bell rang.

Everyone picked up some food in their spoon and then fed the food to the person opposite. Slowly and playfully they fed each other till they were full and satisfied.

'These are the spoons of heaven,' said St Peter.

Sources
and
Resources

This section provides more detail on the various sources I drew upon when first learning to tell any given story. Other variants are also included which may be of interest.

There are picture books and storybooks, which may be used to link the story to reading and research activities in various ways, and also web clips and other web resources for the children to experience as they go deeper into the story.

Lazy Jack

Lazy Jack is another English Folktale collected by Joseph Jacobs (Jacobs, Joseph [1890, 2005] *English Fairy Tales*, Public Domain Books). It is a favourite of English storytellers and there are many picture book versions.

Children's Books

Ross, Tony (1997) *Lazy Jack*, (Puffin Picture Story Book) Puffin Books, imprint of Penguin Books Ltd., London.

French, Vivian; Ayto, Russel (1996) *Lazy Jack*, Walker Books Ltd, London.

Gallagher, Belinda (2011) *Lazy Jack and Other Five- Minute Stories*, Miles Kelly Publishing Ltd., Thaxted, Essex.

Biro, Val (1996) *Lazy Jack*, Oxford University Press, Oxford.

Web Sources

Jacobs, Joseph English Fairy Tales Authorama: http://www.authorama.com/english-fairy-tales-30.html

Guillain, Adam (2009–2013) Story Museum: http://www.storymuseum.org.uk/1001stories/ detail/142/lazy-jack.html

Natasha; Deakin, Claire (Accessed online 17/01/2014) Lazy Jack Storynory: http://www.storynory.com/2008/04/21/lazy-jack/

The Cap of Rushes

This tale is an English Folktale standard, first collected by Joseph Jacobs in the 19th century.

Children's Books

British Broadcasting Corporation (1979) *The Jackanory Story Book*, The Book Club Associates, Norfolk.

Other Print Versions

Jacobs, Joseph (1890, 2005) *English Fairy Tales*, Public Domain Books.

Web Sources

Ashliman, D.L. (1998–2013) Love Like Salt: folktales of types 923 and 510: http://www.pitt.edu/~dash/salt.html

Authorama Public Domain Books/Jacobs, Joseph English Fairy Tales: http://www.
authorama.com/english-fairy-tales-13.html

Marriage of Ganesh

Children's Books

I found this lovely and little known Ganesh story in *The Bronze Cauldron: Myths and
Legends of the World* (McCaughrean, Geraldine [1999] Margaret K. McElderry Books,
imprint of Simon and Schuster, London.) Geraldine McCaughrean kindly gave her
blessing to the retelling in this book. The back- story of how Ganesh got his elephant head
may also be of interest; I recommend Novesky, Amy; Wedman, Belgin K. (2004) *Elephant
Prince: The Story of Ganesh*, Mandala Publishing, Unknown.

Web Sources

Unknown Author (2013) itimes: http://ww.itimes. com/blog/story-of-kartikeya-and-
ganesh-51613cccc51d8

Smith, Chris (2009–2013) Story Museum: http://www.storymuseum.org.uk/1001stories/
detail/97/the-marriage-of-ganesh.html

Smith, Chris (2009–2013) Story Museum: http://www.storymuseum.org.uk/1001stories/
detail/125/how-ganesh-got-married.html

Baba Yaga's Black Geese

I learned this Russian tale from Adam Guillain, who tells the story on the Story Museum
website (Guillain, Adam [2009-2013] Baba Yaga's Black Geese Story Museum: http://
www.storymuseum. org.uk/1001stories/detail/136/baba-yaga-s-black- geese.html).

Children's Books

Lurie, Alison; Souhami, Jessica (2007) *Baba Yaga and the Stolen Baby*, Frances Lincoln
Publishers, London

Sims, Lesley (2010) *Illustrated Stories from Around the World*, Usborne Publishing Ltd, London.

Mayer, Marianna; Craft, K.Y. (1994) *Baba Yaga and Vasilisa the Brave*, William Morrow
and Company Inc., New York.

Other Print Versions

Carter, Angela (2005) Angela Carter's *Book of Fairy Tales*, Virago Press, London.

De Blumenthal, Vera Xenophontovna Kalamatiano (1903) *Folk Tales from the Russian*, Rand McNally and Co., New York.

Web Sources

Barberton, Zan (2012) Baba Yaga and the Black Geese. Vimeo: http://vimeo.com/51125282

Three Brothers and the Polar Bear

While developing a story for a project about global warming, I reset this tale in the arctic. Since then the setting has stuck with me. Originally I know this story as an Indian tale with a lion instead of a polar bear. I first found the tale in a collection of Goblin stories (Ryder, Arthur W. [2008] *22 Goblins*, MacMay22, Unkown).

Other Print Versions

Zimmer, Heinrich (1971) *The King and the Corpse: Tales of the Soul's Conquest of Evil*, Motilal Banarsidass Publishing.

Web Sources

Smith, Chris (2009–2013) The Three Brothers

Story Museum: http://www.storymuseum.org.uk/1001stories/detail/106/the-three-brothers.html

Lupton, Hugh (2013) The Cow-Tail Switch Youtube: http://www.youtube.com/watch?v=Dvse_vHQ9vo

Three Dolls

Most versions of this tale use a King as the main protagonist. I have chosen to reset the tale in a school to illustrate the relevance of its message to the Storytelling School's model for education. It sums up the value of storytelling so well! I first read this tale in *Ready-to-Tell-Tales*, (Novak, David; Holt, David; Mooney, Bill [1994], August House Inc., Atlanta.). David Novak reports hearing it from an Indian storyteller, Mr. Dasgupta.

Web Sources

Smith, Chris (2009–2013) The Three Dolls Story Museum: http://www.storymuseum. org.uk/1001stories/detail/98/the-three-dolls.html

Heathfield, David (Accessed online 17/01/2014) The Three Dolls WorldStories: http:// www.worldstories.org.uk/stories/story/36-the-three-dolls

Morganschatzblackrose (2013) The Three Dolls Wordpress: http://morganschatzblackrose. wordpress.com/2013/05/01/the-three-dolls/

Bhagavân S'rî Sathya Sai Baba (Accessed online 17/01/2014) The Three Dolls helloyou: http://askbaba.helloyou.ch/stories/s1004.html

Al-Mukhtar Standard Schools (2013) Secret of the Three Dolls Youtube: http://www. youtube.com/watch?v=Y6gapQG8_fg

Taletimestories (2013) The Three Dolls: A Story about Storytelling tes: http://www.tes. co.uk/ teaching-resource/The-Three-Dolls-A-Story-about- Storytelling-6316374/

The Lighthouse Keeper and the Selkie

Scottish Lore is full of tales where a seal becomes a wife and then later returns to the sea. I can't remember where I first heard this one, though it is often referred to as *The Selkie Bride*. For further sources and resources see also *The Woman of the Sea*.

Web Sources

Unknown (Accessed online 17/01/2014) The Selkie Bride: A Scottish Folktale WeinGartDesign: http://www.weingartdesign.com/TMaS/Stories/tmas1-SelkieBride.html

McCrorie, Walter (2011) The Selkie Bride Youtube: http://www.youtube.com/watch?v=vQ M2nGpMrtU

Black, Frank (2010) The Selkie Bride Youtube: http://www.youtube.com/watch?v=vm WNBtJU2u8

Muir, Tom Story of a Selkie Education Scotland: http://www.educationscotland.gov.uk/ scotlandsstories/aselkiestory/index.asp

Towrie, Sigurd (1996–2013) The Goodman O' Wastness Orkney Jar: http://www. orkneyjar.com/folklore/selkiefolk/wastness.htm

Death in a Nutshell

I first heard this story from Jane George of Coral Arts, Oxford. My retelling is similar to this and to the Norwegian version, which can be found in *Norwegian Folktales*, (Asbjørnsen, Peter Christen; Moe, Jørgen; Werenskiold, Erik; Kittelsen, Theodor; Shaw, Pat; Norman, Carl [1982] *Norwegian Folktales*, Pantheon Books, a division of Random House Inc., New York).

Children's Books

Maddern, Eric; Hess, Paul (2005) *Death in a Nut*, Frances Lincoln Publishers, London.

Williamson, Duncan (2013) *The Flight of the Golden Bird: Scottish Folktales for Children*, Floris Books, Edinburgh.

Web Sources

Smith, Chris (2009-2013) Death in a Nutshell Story Museum: http://www.storymuseum.org.uk/1001stories/detail/123/death-in-a-nutshell.html

The Fox and the Healer

I first heard this from storyteller Ashley Ramsden at Emerson College. Later I read it in *Tales of Wisdom and Wonder* (Lupton, Hugh; Sharkey, Niamh [1998], Barefoot Books Ltd., Oxford).

Hugh Lupton cites Howard Norman (Norman, Howard [1982] *Where the Chill Came From: Cree Windigo Tales and Journeys*, North Point Press, San Francicso.). Hugh Lupton kindly gave me permission to publish this retelling.

Web Sources

Allison, Daniel. The Fox in the Snow Among the Wild Deer: http://www.amongthewilddeer.com/thefoxinthesnow/

Jack and the Dancing Trees

This story is also known by the name *Auld Cruivie*.

Web Sources

Robinson, Stanley Auld Cruivie Education Scotland: http://www.educationscotland.gov.uk/scotlandsstories/auldcruivie/

McNicol, Claire (2013) blogspot: http://nicerailittleblog.blogspot.co.uk/2013/05/auld-cruivie-or-jack-and-dancing.html

Little Burnt Face

This story is sometimes known as *The Algonquin Cinderella*, as well as variations on *Sootface* or *The Rough-Face Girl*. It is a Micmac Native American Tale.

Children's Books

Martin, Rafe; Shannon, David (1992) *The Rough-Face Girl*, Putnam Berkley Group Inc., New York.

San Souci, Robert D.: San Souci, Daniel (1994) *Sootface*, Bantam Doubleday Dell Publishing Group Inc., New York.

Johnson, Edna; Scott, Carrie (1935) *Anthology of Children's Literature*, Houghton Mifflin Co., Boston.

Lock, Kath; Kennet, David (1997) *Little Burnt Face*, Era Publications Pty, Brooklyn Park, Australia.

Olcott, Frances Jenkins (1917, 2006) *The Red Indian Fairy Book*, Houghton Mifflin Co., Boston. *Republished Yesterday's Classics*, LLC, Unkown.

Other Print Versions

Shah, Idries (1979) *World Tales*, Penguin Books Ltd., London.

Web Sources

Shepard, Aaron (1996) The Hidden One Aaron Shep: http://www.aaronshep.com/stories/046.html

Unknown (Accessed online 17/01/2014) Little Burnt Face: A Micmac Tale from North America Sur LaLune: http://www.surlalunefairytales.com/cinderella/stories/littleburntface.html

The Monk and the Thieves

My source for this was Saviour Pirotta's retelling (Pirotta, Saviour; Johnson, Richard [2007] *Around the World in 80 Tales*, Kingfisher Publications Plc., London.)

The Story Bag

I first heard this told by storyteller Daniel Morden in one of his amazing shows full of music and stories. It is a storytelling favourite, with dozens of versions all over the internet.

Other Print Versions

So-Un, Kim; Eui-Hwan, Kim; Higashi, Setsu (1989) *The Story Bag: A collection of Korean Folk Tales*, Tuttle Publishing, North Clarendon.

In-Sob, Zong (1952) *Folk Tales from Korea*, Routledge and Kegan Paul, London.

King, Nancy R.; Gersie, Alida (1989) *Storymaking in Education and Therapy*, Jessica Kingsley Publishers Ltd., London.

Web Sources

Zun, Mun Czang; Mimi The Storyteller (2011) The Story Spirits youtube: http://www.youtube.com/watch?v=SVnGGh7DccI

Ehrmen, Kelly (2013) The Bag Full of Stories Lavender's Blue Home School: http://lavendersbluehomeschool.com/story-the-bag-full-of-stories/

How a Boy Learned to be Wise

I found this story in an amazing collection of stories from Uganda: Baskerville, Mrs. George; Morris, Mrs. E. G. (1922, 2008) *The King of the Snakes and Other Folk-Lore Stories from Uganda*, The Sheldon Press, London. Reprinted Dodo Press, Gloucester.

Persephone

I first read this as a child in my favourite book of Greek Myths: *The God Beneath the Sea* (Garfield, Leon; Blishen, Edward; Keeping, Charles [1977, 2014), Doubleday Children's, imprint of Random House Children's Publishers UK, London.). There are countless versions in print and online.

Children's Books

McCaughrean, Geraldine: Clark, Emma Chichester (1992) *The Orchard Book of Greek Myths*, Orchard Books, London.

Clayton, Sally Pomme; Lee, Virginia (2009) *Persephone: a Journey from Winter to Spring*, Frances Lincoln Ltd., London

Williams, Marcia (1991) *Greek Myths*, Walker Books, London.

Milbourne, Anna; Stowell, Louie; Temporin, Elena; Bursi, Simona (2010) *Usborne Book of Greek Myths* (Usborne Myths and Legends), Usborne Books, Oxon.

Other Print Versions

Graves, Robert (1995) *Greek Myths*, Penguin Books Ltd., London.

D'Aulaire, Ingri; D'Aulaire, Edgar Parin(1962) *D'Aulaire's Book of Greek Myths*, Delacorte Press, imprint of Random House Inc., New York.

The Wooden Horse

This is another Greek standard. Homer is the main original source (*The Iliad*) of which there are many translations. Hugh Lupton and Daniel Morden have a great show based on the Iliad, in which this story is included.

Children's Books

McCaughrean, Geraldine: Clark, Emma Chichester (1992) *The Orchard Book of Greek Myths*, Orchard Books, London.

Milbourne, Anna; Stowell, Louie; Temporin, Elena; Bursi, Simona (2010) *Usborne Book of Greek Myths* (Usborne Myths and Legends), Usborne Books, Oxon.

Punter, Russel; Pincelli, Matteo (2011) *The Wooden Horse* (Young Reading), Usborne Publishing Ltd, London.

Meister, Cari; Harris, Nick (2012) *Wooden Horse of Troy*, Raintree Publishing, Basingstoke Hants.

Pirotta, Saviour; Lewis, Jan (2006) *Odysseus and the Wooden Horse* (First Greek Myths), Orchard Books, London.

Other Print Versions

Graves, Robert (1995) *Greek Myths*, Penguin Books Ltd., London.

Half a Blanket

I first read this story in a Scottish version by Maggi Pierce in *Ready-to-Tell-Tales* (Peirce, Maggi Kerr; Holt, David; Mooney, Bill [1994, August House Inc., Atlanta.) It turns up in all sorts of places: below there is a Jewish version, a Native American version and a Medieval European version.

Other Print Versions

Schram, Peninnah (2008) *The Hungry Clothes and Other Jewish Folktales*, Sterling Publishing, New York.

Web Sources

Jordan, Elaine Marie (2002–2013) The Divided Horsecloth Tradition In Action: http://www.traditioninaction.org/religious/h032rp.Horsecloth_Jordan.html

Takatoka (2010) This Blanket is for You Manataka: http://www.manataka.org/page2356.html

Fruit of Love

I first heard this told by the Native American storyteller extraordinaire Michael Moran.

Children's Books

Bruchac, Joseph; Vojtech, Anna (1998) *The First Strawberries: A Cherokee Story* (Picture Puffins), Puffin Books, Penguin Putnam Books for Young Readers, New York.

Other Print Versions

Mooney, James (1900, 2003) *Myths of the Cherokee*, Dover Publications Inc., Unknown.

Web Sources

Traditional (Accessed online 17/01/2014) Strawberry Legend First People: http://www.firstpeople.us/FP-Html-Legends/StrawberryLegend-Cherokee.html

Brill, Steve (Accessed online 17/01/2014) The Origin of Strawberries Wild Man Steve Brill: http://www.wildmanstevebrill.com/Plants.Folder/Strawberry.html

Warren, Barbara Shining Woman (Accessed online 17/01/2014) The First Strawberries Powersource: http://www.powersource.com/cocinc/articles/strwbry.htm

Unkown (Accessed online 17/01/2014) The Origin of Strawberries: A Native American Folktale Blogspot: http://storytellingcookingandkids.blogspot.co.uk/2010/06/origin-of-strawberriesa-native- american.html

Smith, Chris (2009-2013) Fruit of Love Story Museum: http://www.storymuseum.org.uk/1001stories/detail/207/the-fruit-of-love.html

One Wish

This is a great little Irish tale, rather like a riddle tale and very popular with teachers and storytellers.

Short and satisfying! The commonly told story involves three problems: wanting a baby, restoring the sight of a mother and having more money.

My own version is an example of story innovation, recycling the original plot with a footballing twist. Very different from, say, the version where Ganesh is the wish granter.

Web Sources

Bukowiec, Annette (2012) One Wish, Irish Folktale Blogspot: http://geowonderland.blogspot.co.uk/2012/03/one-wish-irish-folktale.html

Chowdhury, Rohini (Accessed online 17/01/2014) How the Old Woman Got Her Wish Long Long Time Ago: http://www.longlongtimeago.com/llta_folktales_oldwomanwish.html

Smith, Chris (2009–2013) One Wish Story Museum: http://www.storymuseum.org.uk/1001stories/detail/129/one-wish.html

Moss, Adele (2009–2013) The Wise Wish Story Museum: http://www.storymuseum.org.uk/1001stories/detail/118/the-wise-wish.html

Birth of Athena

I first read this story as a child in my favourite book of Greek Myths: *The God Beneath the Sea* (Garfield, Leon; Blishen, Edward; Keeping, Charles [1977, 2014], Doubleday Children's, imprint of Random House Children's Publishers UK, London.). There are countless versions in print and online. More collections of Greek Myths can be found in the sources for *Persephone*.

Children's Books

Milbourne, Anna; Stowell, Louie; Temporin, Elena; Bursi, Simona (2010) *Usborne Book of Greek Myths* (Usborne Myths and Legends), Usborne Books, Oxon.

Other Print Versions

Graves, Robert (1995) *Greek Myths*, Penguin Books Ltd., London.

D'Aulaire, Ingri; D'Aulaire, Edgar Parin(1962) *D'Aulaire's Book of Greek Myths*, Delacorte Press, imprint of Random House Inc., New York.

Deacy, Susan (2008) *Athena*, Routledge, Oxon.

The Lode Stone

I cannot remember where I first heard this one, except that it was in Eric Maddern's wood in Wales and I haven't found any other sources yet!

Web Sources

Smith, Chris (2009–2013) The Lode Stone Story Museum: http://www.storymuseum.org.uk/1001stories/detail/205/the-lode-stone.html

The Scorpion and the Frog

I first heard this story from Ashley Ramsden at Emerson College; he used it as a powerful metaphor for the dangers of anger. This fable is known by other names, including *The Scorpion* and *The Turtle and Kalil and Dumina*, and can be found in *Aesop's Fables* as well as collections of the *Panchatatra*, which is a collection of ancient Hindu Fables. This story also turns up in the 1992 film *The Crying Game*, when a prisoner uses it to explain how he ended up in prison.

Children's Books

Publisher, Phantom; Odu, Tn (2010) *The Lady Frog and The Scorpion*, Phantom House Books Ltd., Nigeria.

Other Print Versions

Sarma, Visnu; Rajan, Chandra (1993, 2006) *Panc'atantra*, Penguin Classics, Penguin Books Ltd., London.

Web Sources

Unknown, The Scorpion and the Frog Short Stories: http://shortstoriesshort.com/story/the-scorpion-and-the-frog/

Three Wishes

There are so many versions of this story featuring various misguided wishes, and many can easily be found online.

Children's Books

Melling, David (2007) *The Three Wishes*, Hodder Children's Books, London.

Sims, Lesley; Squillace, Eilsa (2009) *The Three Wishes*, Usborne Publishing Ltd., London.

Harrison, Joanna (2000) *The Three Wishes*, HarperCollins, London.

Other Print Versions

Sylvester, Doug (1987) *Folkfest: Folktales from Around the World*, Rainbow Horizons Publishing, San Diego.

Djurklou, Nils Gabriel; Braekstad, H, L. (1901) *Fairy Tales from the Swedish*, J. B. Lippincott Company, Philadelphia and New York.

The Blind Man and the Hunter

This is a story with many sources; Alexander McCall Smith's version, titled *Blind Man Catches a Bird*, can be found in *The Girl Who Married a Lion and Other Tales From Africa* (Smith, Alexander Mccall [1989, 1999, 2004], Random House Inc., New York.). Alexander McCall Smith attributes this story as an Ndebele tale from Zimbabwe. There is also a version by Hugh Lupton, who says that he heard the story from Duncan Williamson.

Children's Books

Lupton, Hugh; Sharkey, Niamh (1998) *Tales of Wisdom and Wonder*, Barefoot Books, Oxford.

Other Print Versions

Macdonald, Margaret Read (1992) *Peace Tales*, August House Inc., Atlanta.

Web Sources

Lupton, Hugh (2009–2013) The Blind Man and the Hunter Story Museum: http://www. storymuseum.org.uk/1001stories/detail/155/the-blind-man-and-the-hunter.html

Unknown (2007) A Blind Man Catches a Bird Wordpress: http://littleganeshas.wordpress. com/2007/05/31/a-blind-man-catches-a-bird/

Timpanelli, Gioia A Blind Man Catches a Bird PRX: http://www.prx.org/pieces/91629-a-blind-man-catches-a-bird-description

Rhino Girl; Frankel, Nina; Wood, Noah (2013) The Blind Man and The Hunter Fight For Rhinos: http://fightforrhinos.com/2013/04/11/the-blind-man-and- the-hunter/

The Birth of Osiris

I first read this story in the lovely picture book *Egyptian Myths* (Morley, Jacqueline; Casselli, Giovanni [1999], Peter Bedrick Books, New York).

Children's Books

Coley, Mike; Alston, Nick (2013) *Osiris*, Bellykids, Unkown (UK)

Other Print Versions

Tyldesley, Joyce (2010) *Myths and Legends of Ancient Egypt*, Penguin Books Ltd., London.

Web Sources

Unknown (2005–2010) The Children of Nut the Lady of Heaven: http://www.legends. egyptholiday.com/ children_of_nut.htm

Furst, Dan (2001) The Stories of Thoth and Ma'at: http://www.hermes3.net/thoth6.htm

Prometheus

Again, as with many of the Greek Myths in this book, I first came across this as a child in *The God Beneath the Sea* (Garfield, Leon; Blishen, Edward; Keeping, Charles [1977, 2014] Doubleday Children's, imprint of Random House Children's

Publishers UK, London.). *Prometheus* retellings can be found in countless collections.

Children's Books

McCaughrean, Geraldine: Clark, Emma Chichester (1992) *The Orchard Book of Greek Myths*, Orchard Books, London.

Williams, Marcia (1991) *Greek Myths*, Walker Books, London.

Milbourne, Anna; Stowell, Louie; Temporin, Elena; Bursi, Simona (2010) *Usborne Book of Greek Myths* (Usborne Myths and Legends), Usborne Books, Oxon.

Other Print Versions

Graves, Robert (1995) *Greek Myths*, Penguin Books Ltd., London.

D'Aulaire, Ingri; D'Aulaire, Edgar Parin(1962) *D'Aulaire's Book of Greek Myths*, Delacorte Press, imprint of Random House Inc., New York.

Web Sources

Baldwin, James (1895, reissued 2006) *Old Greek Stories*, Dodo Press, Slough. Available online at: http://www.authorama.com/book/old-greek-stories.html

The Eagle Who Thought He Was A Chicken

I can't remember where I first heard this great little story, which can be found in many different versions. It is often attributed as a Native American story, although African versions have also been published. There are many retellings on the web, as this story is often used as a parable for fulfilling your potential.

Children's Books

Gregowski, Christopher; Daly, Niki; Tutu, Desmond (2000) *Fly, Eagle, Fly!*, Frances Lincoln Ltd., London.

Web Sources

Larson, Jonathan P. (2011) The Eagle Who Thought He Was A Chicken Youtube: http://www.youtube.com/watch?v=4JtOlRmLbMk

Smith, Chris (2009–2013) The Eagle Who Thought He Was A Chicken Story Museum: http://www. storymuseum.org.uk/1001stories/detail/208/the- eagle-who-thought-he-was-a-chicken.html

Somaiah, Rosemarie (2001) The Eagle Who Thought He Was A Chicken Spoken Stories: http://www.spokenstories.org/the-eagle-who-thought-he-was-a- chicken/

How Butterflies Came To Be

Storyteller Michael Moran told me this Native American Papago tale, which went by the name *Why Butterflies are Silent*. I have emphasized the joy rather than the silence in my retelling.

Children's Books

Bruchac, Joseph; Caduto, Michael J. (1991) *Keepers of the Animals: Native American Wildlife Stories and Activities for Children*, Fulcrum Publishing Inc., Colorado.

Other Print Versions

Erdoes, Richard; Ortiz, Alfonso (1984) *American Indian Myths and Legends*, Pantheon Books, Random House Inc., New York.

McCarthy, Tara (1992) *Multicultural Fables and Fairytales*, Scholastic Inc., New York.

Web Sources

Unknown How the Butterflies Came to Be First People: http://www.firstpeople.us/FP-Html-Legends/HowTheButterfliesCameToBe-Papago.html

Sanjit How Butterflies Came to Be Planet Oz Kids: http://www.planetozkids.com/oban/legends/how-butterflies-came-to-be.htm

Conner, Buck (2006–2013) Butterflies Butterfly Pages: http://www.butterflypages.com/stories.php

The Shepherd's Dream

I love this Irish story, with its curious puzzle solving and potential to prompt fascinating discussions about life, dreams and souls.

Children's Books

Lupton, Hugh; Sharkey, Niamh (1998) *Tales of Wisdom and Wonder*, Barefoot Books, Oxford.

Other Print Versions

O'Sullivan, Sean; Dorson, Richard M. (1974) *Folktales of Ireland*, The University of Chicago Press, London and Chicago.

Crossley-Holland, Kevin (1985) *Folktales of the British Isles*, Pantheon Books, a division of Random House Inc., New York.

Web Sources

Smith, Chris (2009–2013) The Shepherd's Dream Story Museum: http://www.storymuseum.org.uk/1001stories/detail/200/the-shepherd-s-dream. html

The Piper's Boots

This cracking yarn, sometimes called *The Piper's Revenge*, has spread throughout the UK storytelling community. I can't remember where I first heard it. You can find a print version by Bill Teare in *More Ready-to-Tell Tales From Around the World* (Teare, Billy; Holt, David; Mooney, Bill [2000], August House Inc., Atlanta.). Billy Teare kindly gave me permission to publish my retelling.

Other Print Versions

O'Lochlainn, Colm (1965) *More Irish Street Ballads*, Pan Books, London.

Pearson, Maggie (2002) *Short and Shocking!*, Oxford University Press, Oxford.

Trevor, William (1989, reissued 2010) *The Oxford Book of Irish Short Stories*, Oxford University Press, Oxford.

Web Sources

Jacob-McDowell, Barra (2013) Why The Piper *Had* To Take His Revenge Blogspot: http://adventuresinbarding.blogspot.co.uk/2013/03/why-piper-had-to-take-his-revenge.html

Midas' Wish and Midas and Apollo

These two tales of Midas are much told. I really love the Ted Hughes retelling in *Tales from Ovid* (Hughes, Ted [1997], Faber and Faber Ltd., London). It's great to listen to him on CD if you get the chance.

Children's Books

Demi (2002) *King Midas: The Golden Touch*, Margaret K. McElderry Books, imprint of Simon and Schuster Children's Publishing Division, New York.

Coats, Lucy; Lewis, Anthony (2002) *Atticus the Storyteller's 100 Greek Myths*, Orion Publishing Group Ltd., London.

Milbourne, Anna; Stowell, Louie; Temporin, Elena; Bursi, Simona (2010) *Usborne Book of Greek Myths* (Usborne Myths and Legends), Usborne Books, Oxon.

McCaughrean, Geraldine: Clark, Emma Chichester (1992) *The Orchard Book of Greek Myths*, Orchard Books, London.

Craft, Charlotte; Craft, Kinuko Y. (1999) *King Midas and the Golden Touch*, William Morrow and Company Inc., New York.

Sims, Lesley; Gordon, Carl; Gordon, Mike (2009) *King Donkey Ears*, Usborne Publishing Ltd., London.

Other Print Versions

Ovid; Raeburn, David; Feeney, Denis (2004) *Metamorphoses: A New Verse Translation*, Penguin Books Ltd., London.

Graves, Robert (1995) *Greek Myths*, Penguin Books Ltd., London.

D'Aulaire, Ingri; D'Aulaire, Edgar Parin(1962) *D'Aulaire's Book of Greek Myths*, Delacorte Press, imprint of Random House Inc., New York.

Theseus and The Minotaur

My main source for developing this story was Robert Graves' *Greek Myths* (Graves, Robert [1995], Greek Myths, Penguin Books Ltd., London.)

Children's Books

McCaughrean, Geraldine: Clark, Emma Chichester (1992) *The Orchard Book of Greek Myths*, Orchard Books, London.

Milbourne, Anna; Stowell, Louie; Temporin, Elena; Bursi, Simona (2010) *Usborne Book of Greek Myths* (Usborne Myths and Legends), Usborne Books, Oxon.

Williams, Marcia (1991) *Greek Myths*, Walker Books, London.

Milbourne, Anna; Stowell, Louie; Temporin, Elena; Bursi, Simona (2010) *Usborne Book of Greek Myths* (Usborne Myths and Legends), Usborne Books, Oxon.

Coats, Lucy; Lewis, Anthony (2002) *Atticus the Storyteller's 100 Greek Myths*, Orion Publishing Group Ltd., London.

Lupton, Hugh; Morden, Daniel; Henaff, Carole (2013) *Theseus and the Minotaur*, Barefoot Books Ltd., Oxford.

Other Print Versions

D'Aulaire, Ingri; D'Aulaire, Edgar Parin(1962) *D'Aulaire's Book of Greek Myths*, Delacorte Press, imprint of Random House Inc., New York.

Web Sources

Baldwin, James (1895, reissued 2006) *Old Greek Stories*, Dodo Press, Slough. Available online at: http://www.authorama.com/book/old-greek- stories.html

Icarus

Icarus is a popular fable for primary schools with its clear lessons and potential for dramatization. Personally I love Ted Hughes' retelling in *Tales from Ovid* (Hughes, Ted [1997], Faber and Faber Ltd., London).

Children's Books

Pirotta, Saviour; Lewis, Jan (2006) *The Boy Who Could Fly* (First Greek Myths), Orchard Books, London.

Williams, Marcia (1991) *Greek Myths*, Walker Books, London.

Milbourne, Anna; Stowell, Louie; Temporin, Elena; Bursi, Simona (2010) *Usborne Book of Greek Myths* (Usborne Myths and Legends), Usborne Books, Oxon.

McCaughrean, Geraldine: Clark, Emma Chichester (1992) *The Orchard Book of Greek Myths*, Orchard Books, London.

Other Print Versions

Ovid; Raeburn, David; Feeney, Denis (2004) *Metamorphoses: A New Verse Translation*, Penguin Books Ltd., London.

Graves, Robert (1995) *Greek Myths*, Penguin Books Ltd., London.

D'Aulaire, Ingri; D'Aulaire, Edgar Parin(1962) *D'Aulaire's Book of Greek Myths*, Delacorte Press, imprint of Random House Inc., New York.

Web Sources

Henson, Jim; Minghella, Anthony (1987) The Storyteller; Daedalus and Icarus The Jim Henson Company. Available to buy on iTunes: https://itunes.apple.com/us/tv-season/jim-hensons-storyteller-complete/id319062204

Watch an extract on youtube: http://www.youtube.com/watch?v=7yp_igX-sDs

The Woman of the Sea

I am not sure where this one came from; there are many many versions of Selkie stories. Several versions appear under the name *The Goodman of Wastness*.

Children's Books

Riordan, James; Hall, Amanda (1996) *Stories from the Sea*, Barefoot Books Ltd., Bristol.

Doherty, Berlie; Bailey, Sian (1996) *Daughter of the Sea*, Penguin Books Ltd., London.

Other Print Versions

Dennison, W. Traill (1893) *Scottish Antiquary VII (The Goodman of Wastness)*, Edinburgh University Press.

Black, G. F. (1903) *Country Folklore III*, Unknown publisher.

Crossley-Holland, Kevin (1985) *Folktales of the British Isles*, Pantheon Books, imprint of Random House Inc., New York.

Web Sources

Muir, Tom Story of a Selkie Education Scotland: http://www.educationscotland.gov.uk/scotlandsstories/aselkiestory/index.asp

Towrie, Sigurd (1996–2013) Orkney Jar: http://www.orkneyjar.com/folklore/selkiefolk/wastness.htm

Morris, Jackie; Crossley-Holland, Kevin (2011) The Sea Woman Youtube: http://www.youtube.com/watch?v=VeIP3ut9R_U

How Jerusalem Began

This story was reportedly collected in Palestine by a visiting Christian from a Muslim storyteller. It then became popular in Jewish Europe and is now firmly established as a Jewish tale while it is still told by Palestinians. There are now hundreds of versions online. You can read my retelling as a picture book in *One City, Two Brothers* (Smith, Chris; Fronty, Aurelia [2007], Barefoot Books Ltd., Oxford.).

Odysseus and the Cyclops

This story originates with Homer's Odyssey. My primary source for this was Robert Graves' *Greek Myths* (Graves, Robert [1995] Penguin Books Ltd., London.)

Children's Books

Milbourne, Anna; Stowell, Louie; Temporin, Elena; Bursi, Simona (2010) *Usborne Book of Greek Myths* (Usborne Myths and Legends), Usborne Books, Oxon.

McCaughrean, Geraldine: Clark, Emma Chichester (1992) *The Orchard Book of Greek Myths*, Orchard Books, London.

Coats, Lucy; Lewis, Anthony (2002) *Atticus the Storyteller's 100 Greek Myths*, Orion Publishing Group Ltd., London.

Other Print Versions

Ovid; Raeburn, David; Feeney, Denis (2004) *Metamorphoses: A New Verse Translation*, Penguin Books Ltd., London.

The Four Dragons

I first came across this lovely tale in *Dragon Tales: A collection of Chinese Stories* (Wang, Fuyang; Cheng, Shu-Fang [1988], Chinese Literature Press, Beijiing).

Other Print Versions

Life, Man V. (2012) MianJian Gushi *Chinese Folktales*, Amazon eBook.

Web Sources

Unknown (2008–2013) The Four Dragons World of Tales: http://www.worldoftales.com/Asian_folktales/Asian_Folktale_6.html

Scott, David The Legend of the Four Dragons: A Chinese Tale retold Abandoned Towers: http://abandonedtowers.com/stories/the-legend-of-the-four-dragons-a-chinese-fairy-tale-retold/

The Land of the Deep Ocean

There are many variants of this tale involving travel to an ocean land and returning to a later age. Often this story is called Urashimo Taro, and it is sometimes cited as the oldest example of time travel occurring in a story.

Children's Books

Sakade, Florence; Hayashi, Yoshio (2008) *Urashima Taro and Other Japanese Children's Favorite Stories*, Tuttle Publishing, Tokyo.

Other Print Versions

Lear, David (2013) *Urashima Taro and Other Tales*, Firestone Books.

Martin, Rafe (1989) *Ghostly Tales of Japan* (available as CD or book), Yellow Moon Press, America.

Ozaki, Yei Theodora (1903 first publishing, reissued 2007) *Japanese Fairytales*, BiblioBazaar, imprint of Barnes and Noble Inc., New York.

Tyler, Royall (1987) *Japanese Tales*, Pantheon Books, imprint of Random House Inc., New York.

Rama and Sita

The original source for this story is the *Ramayana*, two versions of which are included below.

Children's Books

Clayton, Sally Pomme; Herxheimer, Sophie (2010) *Rama and Sita: Path of Flames*, Frances Lincoln Ltd., London.

Milbourne, Anna; Edwards, Linda (2004) *Stories From India*, Usborne Books, Oxon.

Souhami, Jessica (1997) *Rama and the Demon King*, Frances Lincoln Ltd., London.

Other Print Versions

Nagra, Daljit (2013) *Ramayana: A Retelling*, Faber and Faber Ltd., London.

Valmiki; Sattar, Arshia (2010) *Ramayana*, Penguin Books Ltd., London.

The Building of St Paul's Cathedral

This little tale, often going by the name *The Three Bricklayers* is popular with management trainers and business consultants for obvious reasons.

Web Sources

Asimus, Lindy (2012) The Three Bricklayers Design Business Engineering: http://www.designbusines-sengineering.com/lib_3_bricklayers.htm

Drdebbrown (2009) Job Satisfaction: The Story of the Three Bricklayers intentblog: http://intentblog.com/job-satisfaction-story-three-bricklayers/

Wren, Christopher, Coker, Greg (2012) The Recovering Bricklayer the cathedral institute: http://www.thecathedralinstitute.com/2012/05/13/the-recovering-bricklayer/

Feathers in the Wind

I first heard this story from Doug Lipman on his lovely CD *Milk from the Bull's Horn: Tales of Nurturing Men* (Lipman, Doug [1986], Yellow Moon Press, Cambridge MA.) The story is originally attributed to Rabbi Levi Yitzhak of Berdichev.

Children's Books

Forest, Heather; Cutchin, Marcia (2005) *Feathers*, August House Inc., Atlanta.

Web Sources

Brombacher, Shoshanna (2009) A Pillow Full of Feathers Chabad: http://www.chabad.org/library/article_cdo/aid/812861/jewish/A-Pillow-Full-of-Feathers.htm

Smith, Chris (2009–2013) Feathers in the Wind, Story Museum: http://www.storymuseum.org.

Heaven and Hell [1] and [2]

You can find both these stories in many collections, including: Kornfield, Jack; Feldman, Christina (1991) *Soul Food: Stories to Nourish the Spirit and the Heart,* HarperOne, imprint of Harper Collins Publishers, San Francisco; Owen, Nick (2001) *The Magic of Metaphor,* Crown House Publishing, Carmarthen.

Acknowledgements

The stories in this collection are all traditional stories that have evolved over the centuries by being told and retold over and over again. Behind all these tales stand tens of thousands of storytellers who have adapted the tales to suit their own styles and purposes, all part of the still-evolving story.

Many of these stories are quite popular in England, told by storytellers in schools, festivals and story circles throughout the country. I have told all of these stories myself and tried to bring my own storyteller's voice to the written text. However, doubtless I have picked up phrases and ideas from others, as is the way with traditional stories, so thanks to all the tellers of these tales whom I have seen and heard over the years.

I'd like to name a few storytellers who have been particularly inspiring and influential to me over the years, and whose voices I have no doubt sought to imitate and integrate into my own telling. Thanks to Ben Haggarty, Daniel Morden, Hugh Lupton, Jan Blake, Sally Pomme Clayton, Vergene Gulbenkian and Eric Maddern. Thanks to Lucy and Claire at Hawthorn Press for making the book happen, and in particular to Martin Large for his support and advice. Thanks to the Story Museum, Oxford for generously helping with the editing of earlier drafts of this collection. Much appreciation to Alida Gersie and Hugh Lupton for their advice and feedback when preparing this book.

Finally, I'd like to acknowledge the stories themselves. They come alive when told and retold out loud. They like to be shared, changed, played around with and enjoyed. With your help, may they go forth and multiply.

About the Author

Chris Smith PhD

Chris Smith PhD, is a storyteller, educational trainer and founding Director of Storytelling Schools. Chris loves helping to make education more joyful, effective and engaging, especially in areas of social deprivation where good education can make such a difference to future life chances. For the last twenty years Chris has been researching and developing the Storytelling Schools idea in UK schools. Chris has also been a father, musician, exhibition designer, performer, monk, UN manager, human ecologist, surfer and writer. He currently divides his time between a home in Gloucestershire and a wood in Devon.

Storytelling Schools™ is an educational method where oral storytelling is placed at the heart of learning. Our model integrates elements from the creative arts and educational sciences into a whole school method in a lively, dynamic and inclusive way. Educators using our method report huge gains in both academic and personal development. In this approach, oracy and creativity provide the springboards for learning both language and subject content across the curriculum. We provide resources, support and training to organisations and individuals wishing to adopt the method.

For more information visit www.storytellingschools.com

Other Titles from Storytelling Schools

The Storytelling Schools Method: Handbook for Teachers

Chris Smith, Adam Guillain & Kate Barron
Foreword by Pie Corbett

The handbook is aimed at early years, primary school and middle school teachers as well as home educators. Students learn to be storytellers, performing pieces as a way of internalising language, structure and meaning in a simple and engaging way.

ISBN: 9798665184807 Paperback, Twinberrow Publishing

147 Storytelling Games and Creative Activities for the Classroom and the Home

Chris Smith PhD & Kate Barron MEd

This collection provides a clear, concise and rich source of ideas for how to learn and play through storytelling. Sections include speaking and listening games, learning to tell a story, drama, movement, music, poetry, writing, story recycling and story creation. The book is suitable for classroom teachers, early years workers, home educators, team leaders and anyone who wants to play around with stories in a creative and engaging way.

ISBN: 9798634803173 Paperback, Twinberrow Publishing

Stories for this Uncertain Time
Tales and Creative Activities for Teachers and Parents to Help Children Adapt

Chris Smith PhD

All around the world children are learning to adapt to the new realities of the COVID-19 pandemic. This story collection will help primary aged children to better understand the science of the pandemic, their own personal responses and the key behaviours that can keep them and their communities safer.

ISBN: 9798649515276 Paperback, Twinberrow Publishing

All books available via: www.storytellingschools.com/bookshop

World Tales for Family Storytelling
by Chris Smith
from Hawthorn Press

'Carefully collected by Chris Smith, and honed down to perfect gems of storytelling – simple, and memorable, they encourage all of us to become family storytellers.'
Jamila Gavin

These wonderful world tales are all selected from the highly acclaimed *147 Traditional Stories for Primary School Children to Retell*, a reference book used by teachers around the globe. Retelling a story from memory will help your children master new language, ideas and emotions and encourage creativity while building their confidence in communication. In these three books for home use, the stories are to share within your family in whatever way you choose: read them, tell them from memory, change them, re-enact them, discuss them, paint them, play with them and above all get your family to engage with them.

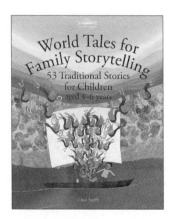

Available Summer 2021
World Tales for Family Storytelling I
53 Traditional Stories for Children aged 4–6 years
ISBN: 978-1-912480-55-5

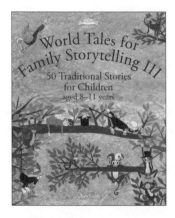

Available Summer 2023
World Tales for Family Storytelling III
50 Traditional Stories for Children aged 8–11 years
ISBN: 978-1-912480-67-8

Other Titles from Hawthorn Press

The Natural Storyteller
Wildlife Tales for Telling
Georgiana Keable

The Natural Storyteller is a vibrant invitation to embrace a world of stories all about nature, animals and plants – and our relationship with them. It includes story maps, brain-teasing riddles, story skeletons and adventures to make a tale your own. This diverse collection of stories will nurture active literacy skills and help form an essential bond with nature. The Natural Storyteller recently won first place in the Green Books/ Environmental category of the Purple Dragonfly Book Awards.

272pp; 228 x 186mm; paperback; ISBN 978-1-907359-80-4

Storytelling with Children
Nancy Mellon

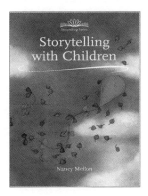

Telling stories is a peaceful, magical way of creating special occasions with children. Nancy believes every parent can, and should, become a confident, creative storyteller, and that stories told by a parent are a gift to your child, a wonderful act of sharing and communicating. Nancy's gentle, practical advice is illustrated with many beautiful, funny and wise stories created by families who have discovered how the power of story transforms lives and relationships.

192pp; 216 x 138mm; paperback; ISBN 978-1-907359-26-2

Storytelling For Nature Connection
Environment, community and story-based learning
Alida Gersie, Anthony Nanson and Edward Schieffelin

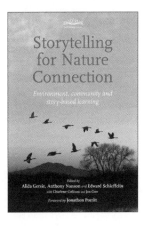

This unique resource offers new ideas, stories, creative activities and methods to encourage pro-environmental behaviour with diverse participants: from people working in conservation, environmental education, youthwork, business training and sustainability. The book enhances participants' emotional literacy and resilience, builds community, and helps people to create a sustainable future together.

376pp; 234 x 156mm; paperback; ISBN 978-1-912480-59-3

An A–Z Collection of Behaviour Tales
From Angry Ant to Zestless Zebra
Susan Perrow

Susan offers story medicine as a creative strategy to help children age 3–9 years face challenges and change behaviour. Following the alphabet, each undesirable behaviour is identified in the story title: anxious, bullying, demanding, fussy, jealous, loud, obnoxious, uncooperative, and more. The stories, some humorous and some serious, are ideal for parenting, teaching and counselling.

144pp; 234 x 156mm; paperback; ISBN 978-1-907359-86-6

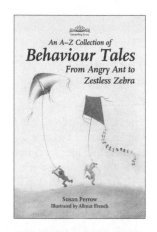

Stories to Light the Night
A Grief and Loss Collection for Children, Families and Communities
Susan Perrow

With a foreword by acclaimed storyteller Alida Gersie , these 94 stories from around the world offer story medicine for children, families and communities at times of grieving, loss and separation, including the loss of nature and ecocide. Stories and words have therapeutic potential. They can strengthen us, help to reframe things, and help make meaning.

192pp; 234 x 156mm; paperback; ISBN 978-1-912480-27-2

Healing Stories for Challenging Behaviour
Susan Perrow

Susan Perrow is a story doctor. She writes, collects and documents stories that offer a therapeutic journey for the storyteller and listener – a positive, imaginative way of healing difficult situations. Healing Stories for Challenging Behaviour is richly illustrated with lively anecdotes drawn from parents and teachers who have discovered how the power of story can help resolve a range of common childhood behaviours and situations such as separation anxiety, bullying, sibling rivalry, nightmares and grieving.

320pp; 234 x 156mm; paperback; ISBN 978-1-903458-78-5

The Children's Forest

Stories & songs, wild food, crafts & celebrations all year round
Dawn Casey, Anna Richardson, Helen d'Ascoli

A rich and abundant treasury in celebration of the outdoors, this book encourages children's natural fascination with the forest and its inhabitants. Full of games, facts, celebrations, craft activities, recipes, foraging, stories and Forest School skills, this book is ideal for ages 5–12, but it will also be enjoyed by adults, families and younger children.

336pp; 200 × 250mm; paperback with flaps; ISBN 978-1-907359-91-0

Making the Children's Year

Seasonal Waldorf Crafts with Children
Marije Rowling

Drawing on the creative ethos of Steiner Waldorf education, this is a full-colour second edition of The Children's Year. Packed with all kinds of seasonal crafts, for beginners and experienced crafters, this book is a gift for parents seeking to make toys that will inspire children and provide an alternative to throwaway culture.

240pp; 250 x 200mm; paperback; ISBN 978-1-907359-69-9

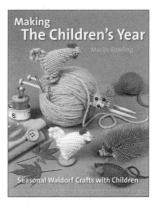

Findus, Food and Fun

Seasonal Crafts and Nature Activities
Eva-Lena Larsson, Kennert Danielsson and Sven Nordqvist

Findus, Food and Fun is for mums, dads, grandparents, teachers, childminders and anyone who knows a young child who is curious about the world. Together with Findus, Pettson and the muckles, you can discover things to do for every season; pottering, collecting, fixing, crafting, building, exploring, baking. Sometimes outdoors, sometimes indoors, here is a whole year's worth of ideas.

64pp; 297 x 210mm; hardback; ISBN 978-1-907359-34-7

Making Peg Dolls

Over 60 fun, creative projects for children and adults
Margaret Bloom

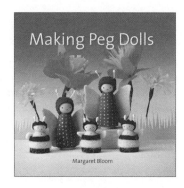

Coming from the Waldorf handcraft tradition, these irresistible dolls encourage creative play and promote the emotional and imaginative development of young children. Easy to follow, step-by-step instructions with beautiful colour illustrations for children and crafters of all levels and experience.

192pp; 200 x 210mm; paperback; ISBN 978-1-907359-77-4

Making Waldorf Crafts

Step-by-step crafts for children from 6 to 8 years
Nina Taylor

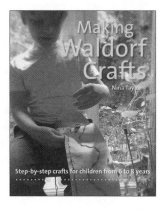

Here is everything you need to encourage small hands to learn sewing, knitting and weaving skills. The author's charming anecdotes and teaching tips alongside the clear illustrations are invaluable for anyone who finds themselves guiding children to learn with their hands. The projects and techniques are accompanied by stories and anecdotes that children won't be able to resist.

128pp; 250 x 200mm; paperback with flaps; ISBN 978-1-912480-39-5

Making Woodland Crafts

Using green sticks, rods, beads and string
Patrick Harrison

This book is guaranteed to get children out and about and enjoying nature. Through a series of stunning hand-drawn illustrations, Making Woodland Crafts provides the basic knowledge and skills to complete a range of both simple and more advanced craft projects.

120pp; 210 x 200mm; paperback; ISBN 978-1-907359-84-2

The Parenting Toolkit (paperback edition)

Simple Steps to Happy & Confident Children
Caroline Penney

Caroline Penney explains clearly how to help your child become confident, capable, caring, and able to reach their full potential. This book also offers tips on how to ensure that you are getting all the self-care that you need in order to be a good parent.

164pp; 250 x 200mm; paperback; ISBN 978-1-912480-11-1

Simplicity Parenting

Using the power of less to raise happy, secure children
Kim John Payne

This is a title for parents who want to slow down, for families with too much stuff, too many choices and too much information. Here are four simple steps for decluttering, quieting, and soothing family dynamics so that children can thrive at school, get along with peers, and nurture well-being.

352pp; 234 x 156mm; paperback; ISBN 978-1-912480-03-6

Between Form and Freedom

Raising a teenager
Betty Staley

Betty Staley's wise guide to raising a teenager includes the stages of adolescence, the search for the self, the birth of the intellect, the release of feelings and male-female differences. Challenges are tackled around self-esteem, pregnancy, behavioural problems, depression, media, genderfluidity, eating disorders, drug and alcohol abuse. Growth needs are explored in relation to family, friends, the media, education, the arts, loyalty and relationships.

368pp; 234 x 156mm; paperback; ISBN 978-1-912480-72-2

All Year Round

A calendar of celebrations

Ann Druitt, Christine Fynes-Clinton, Marije Rowling

Observing the round of festivals is an enjoyable way to bring rhythm into children's lives and provide a series of meaningful landmarks to look forward to. This book is brimming with things to make, activities, stories, poems and songs to share with your family.

320pp; 250 × 200mm; paperback; ISBN 978-1-869890-47-6

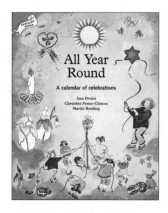

Festivals, Family and Food

Guide to seasonal celebration

Diana Carey, Judy Large

This family favourite is a unique, well-loved source of stories, recipes, things to make, activities, poems, songs and festivals. The perfect present for a family, it explores the numerous festivals that children love celebrating.

224pp; 250 × 200mm; paperback; ISBN 978-0-950706-23-8

Ordering Books

If you have difficulties ordering Hawthorn Press books from a bookshop, you can order direct from our website www.hawthornpress.com, or from our UK distributor BookSource: 50 Cambuslang Road, Glasgow, G32 8NB, Tel: (0845) 370 0063, E-mail: orders@booksource.net.

Details of our overseas distributors can be found on our website.

Hawthorn Press

www.hawthornpress.com